Parakeets

NIKKI MOUSTAKI

Parakeets

Project Team
Editor: Mary E. Grangeia
Technical Editor: Tom Mazorlig
Interior Design: Leah Lococo Ltd. and Stephanie Krautheim
Design Layout: Mary Ann Kahn

T.F.H. Publications
President/CEO: Glen S. Axelrod
Executive Vice President: Mark E. Johnson
Publisher: Christopher T. Reggio
Production Manager: Kathy Bontz

T.F.H. Publications, Inc.
One TFH Plaza Third and Union Avenues
Neptune City, NJ 07753

Discovery Communications, Inc. Book Development Team:
Maureen Smith, Executive Vice President & General
    Manager, Animal Planet
Carol LeBlanc, Vice President, Marketing and
    Retail Development
Elizabeth Bakacs, Vice President, Creative Services
Peggy Ang, Director, Animal Planet Marketing
Caitlin Erb, Marketing Associate

Printed and bound in China
06 07 08 09 10 1 3 5 7 9 8 6 4 2

Library of Congress Cataloging-in-Publication Data
Moustaki, Nikki, 1970-
Parakeets / Nikki Moustaki.
p. cm. – (Animal Planet pet care library)
Includes index.
ISBN 0-7938-3767-7 (alk. paper)
1. Parrots. I. Title. II. Series.
SF473.P3M673 2006
636.6'865–dc22
2006007718

The Leader In Responsible Animal Care For Over 50 Years!™
www.tfhpublications.com

Table of Contents

Chapter 1

Why I Adore My Parakeet 5
A Brief Parakeet History • Physical Characteristics • Temperament
and Behavior • Life Span

Chapter 2

The Stuff of Everyday Life .21
Housing • Furnishings and Accessories

Chapter 3

Good Eating 41
Proper Nutrition • Cooked Diets • Table Foods • Fresh Water •
A Sample Diet • Dietary Supplements

Chapter 4

Looking Good 59
Bathing • Nail Care • Beak Care • Wing Clipping

Chapter 5

Feeling Good 71
Finding an Avian Veterinarian • The Vet Visit • General Signs of
Illness • Common Illnesses • Senior Bird Care

Chapter 6

Being Good 89
Positive Reinforcement • Socialization • Taming • Step-Up and Stick
Training • Talking • Tricks • Problem Behaviors

Resources 104

Index 109

Chapter 1

Why I Adore

My
Parakeet

Parakeets didn't get to be the world's most popular parrot by accident. They are friendly, beautiful, clownish, easy to tame, and they breed readily in captivity.

The average parakeet, also called a budgie, is a slender seven inches (17.8 cm) from his head to his tapered tail and weighs just over one ounce (28.3 g), making him compact enough to keep as an apartment bird. In terms of noise, his loudest calls don't come close to the decibels of other parrots. He might be persistent in his chitter-chatter, but it's not going to disturb the neighbors. The parakeet is loved by fanciers all over the world, as well as being a standard species for beginners to bird keeping because of his hardiness and his manageably sized beak—a bite from another type of parrot is much more formidable. All in all, the parakeet is a loyal, affectionate companion. This book will inform you about the nature of your feathered pal and help you to care for him properly.

A Brief Parakeet History

The bird we call the American parakeet is called a budgie in the rest of the world. The word budgie comes from the aboriginal Australian word for this bird, betchegara (budgerigar), meaning "good to eat." Parakeets are originally from Australia, but the one living in your home was hatched and raised in your country of origin, not caught and imported from the wild. Because the parakeet is so prolific in captivity and has been bred for dozens of years, there's no need to raid wild populations for the pet trade. In any case, it is illegal to import birds into the United States now, so it's a good thing for fanciers that this species has done so well in captivity.

The parakeet enjoys a very wide natural range of the Australian mainland. The wild parakeet is found in large flocks and is highly nomadic, always on the hunt for water, which is scarce in the scrublands, the habitat that makes up much of their natural environment. Parakeets are capable of flying hundreds of miles in search of a water source. They breed in the rainy season when food and water are most

A Parakeet by Any Other Name...

The parakeet is in the parrot family Psittacidae, and though his designation is *keet*, he is a true parrot. The main difference between parrots and parakeets is the tail—most of the birds called *parakeets* have long tapered tails, whereas *parrots* tend to have shorter, blunter tails, although not in every case. A parakeet by any other name is still a parrot.

readily available, nesting in hollowed out trees or on tree limbs. They incubate their eggs, usually 4 to 6 of them, for 16 to 18 days, and then rear chicks for 6 to 8 weeks before the babies are ready to leave the nest.

A bit smaller than domestically bred parakeets, wild parakeets are found in only the wild green, or nominate, color. This color helps them to blend well into their habitat. Hawks and other raptors often prey upon them, so camouflage is extremely important. Their other primary predator is the tree snake.

Wild parakeets consume a variety of plant materials. They feed primarily on the ground and are notorious for raiding farmers' grain fields, making them quite a pest in their native country. Their ability to forage and to go for long periods of time without a good water supply make them hardy birds in captivity, where food and water are abundant. The wild parakeet feeds mainly in the hour just after dawn

and again in the hour just before dusk. This is also the time when your companion parakeet is hungriest. You can capitalize on this natural behavior by feeding the most nourishing foods at this time.

The parakeet's scientific name is *Melopsittacus undulatus*, which roughly translated means "song bird with wavy lines." The common budgie has been known over the years by many different names: American parakeet, English budgie, undulated grass parakeet, shell parakeet, zebra parakeet, and the warbling grass parakeet, just to name a few. Parakeets have even been called lovebirds, but are not to be mistaken with African lovebirds.

Budgies were brought to Europe around 1838 by the British naturalist John Gould and his brother-in-law, Charles Coxen, who is credited with hand-raising the first clutch of wild babies. The new European

The parakeet is one of the most popular companion birds.

In the wild, budgies only come in one color—green, the "nominate" or normal color. All other colors are mutations.

as a companion. Around 1875, a yellow mutation occurred in Belgium, leading to additional new mutations such as olive, dark green, gray-green, and light yellow. Elsewhere, other mutations developed around this time as well: pied, white-blue, and clearwings. Around 1881, a Dutch bird keeper was lucky enough to discover a blue chick in one of his nests. From this blue bird came cobalt, slate, gray, and violet.

budgies bred readily and created quite a fancy among the wealthy in England. After being more widely introduced, other Europeans became enamored with the species, and the bird later became fashionable in Belgium, Holland, France, and Germany as well.

Around 1850, the budgie was displayed at the Antwerp Zoo in Belgium and began to gain in popularity, being bred in such numbers that people other than the very rich were able to enjoy this bird

Importation of budgies into Europe continued until 1894, at which time Australia banned export. Europeans had to then breed their existing stock to be able to continue the hobby. Today, the budgie still enjoys a healthy fancy in Europe, with new mutations being discovered frequently. Breeders in Europe are responsible for the large English budgie, as well as for many of the beautiful budgie colors that we enjoy today.

In 1925, the budgie took off in Japan after a Japanese prince saw a pair of cobalt blue budgies in England and brought them back to his country. This began such a demand for them in Japan that European breeders could hardly supply enough. The Japanese soon began breeding them, resulting in the popular lutino and albino mutations that occurred in the 1930s.

The budgie came to America around the late 1920s, but didn't experience real popularity until the 1950s, when nearly every child had a pet parakeet. Today, there are over seventy recognized color variations stemming from the original wild green Australian budgie. Many other colors exist that aren't even recognized yet. The most recent recognized mutation, the Spangle, occurred in a breeder's aviary in Australia in 1974. Even with the many colors available, most Americans want the most common, basic colors: green, blue, yellow, and white—the colors that you will find in any pet shop. You'll have to look for a breeder or go to a budgie show if you want the fancier more exotic colors.

The Expert Knows

In the Wild

The wild parakeet is an active bird whose days are filled with flying, foraging for food, playing, keeping away from predators, finding nesting sites and nesting, protecting the nest, and raising young. In captivity, your companion parakeet does not have this much to do. Because of the lack of real exercise, companion parakeets are prone to become overweight, which can lead to fatty tumors and a greatly reduced life span. To help your parakeet remain fit and trim, provide him with as much exercise as possible.

Budgie Clubs and Societies

People that love and raise budgies often belong to clubs and societies where like-minded members can get together and learn more about their wonderful birds. These clubs have educational programming, study the breeding habits and mutations, and work to create the "perfect" budgie based on an agreed-upon standard of appearance, much like in dog showing. Generally, these clubs are dedicated to the English show budgie, the larger mutation of the wild parakeet. The English budgie is twice the size of the normal parakeet and has a prominent feathered brow, with eyes that are set back into the feathers on his face. He

In many parts of the world, parakeets are also called budgerigars, or "budgies" for short.

looks a little like a parakeet on steroids! Fanciers breed these birds to show in competitions. They are a little more docile than regular parakeets and make great companions, but they only live half as long. Although their appearance is so different, the parakeet and the English budgie are still the same species.

Physical Characteristics

Parakeets occur in over seventy colors and patterns, called mutations, with more being developed each year. You will probably only find about ten to twelve distinct colors/patterns in your local pet shop. There is no difference in the companionability among the different colors. Blue, green, yellow, white—it's all the same.

In the wild, budgies only come in one color, green, the "nominate" or normal color. The other colors, the mutations, are naturally occurring deviations from the normal color. A wild parakeet that was any color other than green would be an easy mark for a predator, and probably would not live long enough to pass along his genes. In captivity, breeders single out these mutations and breed them widely so that new ones can develop.

Because the normal green is the most common color, it is often the least expensive to purchase. Common mutations, such as lutino (yellow) and blue, are also easily found in pet shops and come with a reasonable price tag. The rare or "fancy" mutations are more difficult to find and come at a higher

English Budgies

Most of the parakeets that you find in pet shops are slender little birds, though others look as if they were put on growth hormones. Those are the English budgies, and though they are often more expensive and shorter lived, they make great companions. These larger show budgies are the result of selective breeding and do not occur in the wild. They are as close to being "domesticated" as any other bird in the parrot family.

price, though there is no difference in companion quality among them all.

Beyond color, the parakeet's body also has many fascinating elements, as you will see in the descriptions that follow.

Eyes

A parakeet's eyes should be round, clear, and bright. There should be no crust or discharge from the eyes. They should show an attitude of alertness. Eye color is either black (in juveniles), very dark with a grey or greenish iris, or red.

Nares and Cere

A parakeet's nostrils are called nares, and they are located on the cere, which is the fleshy part just above the beak. The nares should be clean and without discharge. The cere should not be crusty or peeling. It changes from a pinkish color in the bird's juvenile stage to either blue, if the bird is male, or some variation of pink or brown if the bird is female. The female's cere may become dark brown and crusty when she's in breeding condition, but don't confuse this with scaly face mites, which can also make the cere crusty.

Ears

The parakeet's ears are located just behind the eye toward the back of the

Parakeet IQ

The parakeet is a highly intelligent little bird, able to recognize the people and things in his life. Each one is an individual with his own tastes and personality. Occasionally, you will have to convince him to change his mind—for example, to eat a different food or when it's the right time to take a bath. Parakeets are also chatterboxes and have been reported to say hundreds of words and phrases. Overall, they are affectionate companions that bond readily to humans who are patient and kind to their birds.

Parakeets, or budgies, come in over seventy colors and patterns, with more being developed each year.

head. The ears are covered by fine feathers and look like holes in the bird's head. They are not visible in a healthy adult unless he's wet from bathing. They may be visible in an ill bird that is not well-groomed or is losing feathers.

Feathers

A healthy parakeet's feathers are shiny, tight, and lie flat against the body. A parakeet with ruffled feathers may be ill or temporarily cold. One exception to this is the crested budgie, which has a crest of raised feathers on the top of his head, like a crown. The other exception is the feather duster budgie, which has excessively long feathers, though it is unlikely that you will easily

find one of these for sale. A parakeet with bald patches is either ill, plucking his own feathers, or being plucked by a cagemate. Sometimes, a breeding female will make a "brood patch" on her breast by plucking the feathers there to make a warm spot for the eggs—this is normal.

Feet

A parakeet's feet should be free of debris and nimble enough to perch and climb. Sometimes a parakeet becomes crippled in the nest as a baby and has splayed legs or other foot problems, but can still make a great companion. A parakeet with lame feet still has wings and will be able to get around if allowed to fly. Watch out for crusty, itchy legs and feet, because this can be a sign of mites.

Vent
The vent is the area underneath the bird. It is located at the base of the tail and is the place where waste is eliminated and eggs are laid. The vent area should be clean, not crusted with feces or other material.

Temperament and Behavior
Young parakeets are docile and easily tamed. Once they get older they may come to fear the human hand and may try to flee or bite. Fortunately, the parakeet's beak isn't large, so the bite isn't terrible—but it does hurt. However, even adult parakeets can be tamed with a little time and a lot of patience. In general, they are loyal and affectionate to their human companions, and though they may wander off in search of something good to chew (and probably something inappropriate!), they will rarely turn on a human friend like some other species are prone to do.

A healthy parakeet is active and vocal. Much of his noise sounds like chitter-chatter, and at times like screeching, but it's not loud. Sometimes parakeets sing pretty songs and call one another with whistles. A fit and happy parakeet will be quite noisy, but a silent bird might actually be ill, especially if his cagemates are chirping up a storm. Parakeets even chitter-chatter in their sleep during a daytime nap, but won't make a peep at night when the lights are out. Some people like the chatter and others are driven crazy by the persistence of it. Music is in the ear of the hearer, as they say.

Wild parakeets vocalize consistently around dawn and at

Hardy birds, parakeets make loyal and affectionate companions and are ideal as family pets.

dusk, and then chirp and jibber-jabber pretty much all day long as they go about their business of finding food and courting. Your companion parakeet will do the same. You will not get him to stop vocalizing, but you can choose the time that he begins his daily routine by using a dark cage cover. However, if your parakeet is already used to vocalizing at a certain time of day, it's unlikely that a cover will help. Birds have a very good internal clock and can tell when it's time to get up. If you do use a cage cover, make sure that you wash it with a scent-free detergent and that you dry it without a scented dryer sheet, as these things can irritate your bird's respiratory system.

Parakeets are excellent talkers and will even out-talk most of the larger bird species or parrots. They can learn hundreds of words and phrases and say them clearly and interchangeably.

Good Talkers

If you want a talking parakeet, your best bet is to find a male. Male budgies are the best talkers among parrots in general and have been recorded repeating over a thousand words and phrases. If you do get a female, however, she may pick up a few words and may learn to whistle. If you're buying, look at the cere (fleshy area above the beak)—at about four month of age it begins to change, making it easy to tell the males from females; the rule is blue for boys, pink or brown for girls.

Hand-Fed Babies

If you want to buy a hand-tamed parakeet, try to find a breeder that hand-feeds his or her babies. This means that the breeder will take the baby away from the parents when it is still reliant on them and take over their parental duties. It's tough to find a hand-fed baby in a pet shop because most breeders don't bother hand-feeding and weaning parakeets, but you may be able to find a breeder that will do it for you.

Males are more apt to talk earlier and more frequently than females, but hens have been known to do their fair share as well. Both can whistle with equal facility.

As far as intelligence goes, the parakeet is no birdbrain. This little bird is able to recognize and distinguish the people and objects in his life. Each parakeet is an individual, with his own preferences and dislikes. There is anecdotal evidence to show that some can even speak in context, like several larger birds, and can associate human language with objects the way we do. For example, if he wants a cracker he might ask for one—perhaps he's not just repeating "wannna cracker" just because he has been trained to do so or has heard it often.

As for basic behavior, parakeets are generally active and perky. A bird sitting on the bottom of the cage, fluffed and sleepy, might be ill or injured. Healthy parakeets are generally wandering around the cage socializing, eating, and bathing. The one in the corner on the bottom of the cage is trying to take a "time out" and get away from the others because he doesn't feel well or is being picked on.

Most birds like to perch in the highest spot possible, because a high place makes a secure lookout point. Birds are prey animals and are always on the lookout for predators. You may find that your parakeet stops vocalizing when your dog or cat enters the room, or becomes agitated when he sees a hawk overhead, even if there's a window between the predator and your bird. Because wild parakeets forage on the ground, they are highly sensitive to sound and movement.

Being in a high spot isn't the only behavioral instinct that your companion parakeet will exhibit. Even a single bird has the natural instinct to breed and will try to do so with a toy, a coop cup, or his owner's hand. A parakeet that is stimulated to breed may also become cranky and nippy. In the wild, parakeets breed when

Well-known for their vocalizations, parakeets frequently talk, sing, and mimic words and sounds.

there's an abundance of light, food, and water. Your parakeet has the same programming. If he does not give up his breeding behavior, cut down the amount of light he receives to about nine or ten hours a day, serve water in a smaller cup (to discourage bathing for a short time), and remove the toy or cup that your parakeet believes is his mate. When the clocks change in the fall, you can go back to bathing your bird, and his or her behavior should return to normal. Or, better yet, get your parakeet a companion, not to encourage breeding (don't offer a nesting area), but to alleviate the frustration of not having a friend.

Life Span

A parakeet can live to be 12 to 15 years old, or more with appropriate care and diet. The larger English budgie can live to be about 7 or 8. By the time you buy your bird, he will probably be at least two months old and eating on his own. This is the best time to get a parakeet if you want it to be tame. Most baby parakeets are eating fine on their own at 6 to 8 weeks of age and can be taken to a new home. Some breeders wait a little longer before they sell the babies to make certain they're strong and healthy. Parakeets reach young adulthood at about 6 to 9 months of age. If you get an adult that has never been handled by humans, you will have to spend more time taming him.

There are four reliable ways to tell the age of your parakeet: You can examine his head barring, eyes, and cere and, in some cases, look for information supplied on a leg band.

Leg Band

A closed band is generally put on the leg by the breeder when the parakeet is a hatchling, and it is engraved with his initials, state, and the month and year in which the

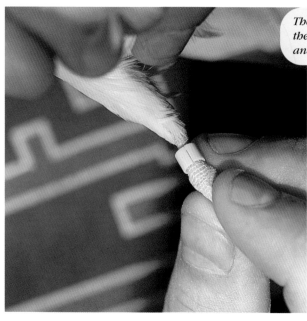

on their backs, with the exception of albinos (white) and lutinos (yellow), which don't have stripes at all. This head-barring disappears as the bird grows older and is replaced by a solid color. Once the bars are gone, however, it's hard to tell a three-year-old bird from an eight-year-old bird, unless it is wearing a leg band.

17

bird was hatched. This is the only reliable way to tell the age of a parakeet.

Head Barring

Baby parakeets have the same bar stripes on their heads that they have

Eyes

The eyes of a very young parakeet are all black. The iris lightens as the bird gets older, and you can see the

Leg Bands

Most states require breeders selling birds to put a closed band on one of the birds' legs before he can be sold. Engraved into it are the initials of the breeder, the state where the bird was bred, the year the bird was hatched, and a number that is unique to your individual bird. This last number helps the breeder keep records of the babies. Some people have this band removed, especially if it is irritating the bird or there is a chance that the band will become caught on something in the cage or aviary, causing the leg to break or the skin to tear. Do not ever try to remove this band yourself. Your avian veterinarian or local bird shop has a special tool to remove it.

Why I Adore My Parakeet

Long-Term Care

Your parakeet may live 12 to 15 years, so you must be willing to make a long-term commitment to your bird. Even if a child promises to feed and tend to his or her pet, the adults in the household must ultimately take on responsibility for the animal's care. A child may forget to feed the animal, and in the case of a parakeet, that can be deadly. So, be ready for the following responsibilities:

- Daily cage cleaning.
- Weekly perch scrubbing.
- Offering fresh water twice daily.
- Offering and changing fresh foods daily.
- Conducting safe playtime out of the cage daily.
- Watching for signs of illness and taking your parakeet to the veterinarian if you suspect something is wrong or in the event of an accident.
- Parakeet-proofing your home.
- Watching other pets closely when the bird is out of his cage.
- Making sure that the cage is out of drafts and that it doesn't get too cold or too warm in the bird's environment.
- Checking the cage and toys daily for dangerous wear and tear.

dark pupil in the center. However, albino and lutino parakeets have red eyes, so you can't tell their age by the color of their eyes.

The Cere

The cere is the fleshy area just above the beak. This fleshy spot

Parakeets are very social, intelligent birds, so you must be willing to commit to the time and attention their care requires.

is very blue in adult males and very pink or brown in adult females. In baby parakeets, the cere is whitish, pinkish, and/or bluish, an indefinite color indicating that the bird is still young. Again, this method doesn't work with albinos and lutinos because the cere in both sexes is light in color.

Chapter 2

The Stuff of

Everyday Life

Once you've gotten your parakeet, you'll need to invest in a few essential items to keep him healthy and content. It may seem like a long list, but these are really just the basics.

It is important that you have everything ready for your parakeet when he arrives so that he can immediately feel comfortable and secure.

your decision, they should not be the sole deciding factors in buying a cage. Remember, your parakeet will be spending considerable time in his new home. A cage should be your parakeet's home, not his prison.

Square or rectangular cages are a better choice than round ones. Your parakeet will like a corner to scrunch into, and a round cage does not offer that option. Square or rectangular cages also offer more space for the same basic cage size. Also, some round cages have bars that taper toward the top, which can be a choking hazard should the bird get his neck caught between the bars. Tapered bars can also catch a nail and cause it or the toe to break.

Some people think that they're not going to have a cage at all, and that the bird will live in the house or in a certain room. This might sound good in theory, but it's simply not practical or safe to have your bird flying around the house twenty-four hours a day. He

Housing

As you've probably noticed from going to the pet shop or your favorite e-commerce pet retailer, there are many types of cage on the market. Some of them are even labeled "parakeet cages." But which one is right for your bird?

The housing decision might appear obvious. Perhaps you want a certain color, or you have budget restrictions. Though these things can influence

Bigger is Better

A parakeet's cage should be as large and roomy as possible. It should be big enough to accommodate perches, food dishes, and toys, while still allowing your bird some space for flying.

needs a place to rest, eat, and play. It's true that birds don't really belong in cages, but for the house parakeet, the home presents a great deal of hazards that can be avoided by providing him with his own safe haven.

Cage Size

Some cages are labeled for parakeets, usually small, pastel colored enclosures that are geared toward the décor of a child's room. This is an unacceptable home for your parakeet, unless, however, he is out of his cage and interacting with you for most of the day. In any other case, you should buy a much larger cage. One that's labeled "flight cage" or "cockatiel cage" is probably a better choice than the tiny varieties most stores sell for parakeets. In a perfect world, the very minimum size would be 36 in. (91.4 cm) wide x 24 in. (61 cm) deep x 48 in. (121.9 cm) tall. Buy a cage even larger than this if you can.

Even though a cage is nice and roomy, it may not be safe for a parakeet. Make certain that the bars are not wide enough for the bird to stick his head through, which can cause him to panic and injure himself, perhaps fatally. The bar spacing should be no more than 1/2 to 5/8 inch (1.27-1.59 cm).

Cage Materials

When shopping for cages, think of practicality, comfort, and appropriate features first. The cosmetics of the cage should be secondary. A pretty cage is not always the best or safest home for your parakeet. Fortunately, manufacturers have gotten savvy in the

Flying Right

Flying is wonderful exercise, perfectly suited for birds, but it's not always advisable to have a parakeet flying inside the average home. With his wing feathers clipped, he can get exercise from flapping, playing with toys, climbing ropes and ladders, and plenty of playtime out of the cage with his owners; however, flying is ideal. Walking around on the floor might seem like good exercise, but there's a risk that your parakeet can be stepped on (especially if your carpet and your parakeet are similar in color), or could become a snack for the family dog or cat.

Rectangular or square cages are the best type of housing because they offer more security and space than round enclosures.

past few years and are designing more attractive cages with both décor and safety in mind.

Most are made of metal and plastic, and some are coated with paint to add color and texture. Powder-coated cages are made by spraying the bars with a specific type of powdered paint, and then using high temperatures to melt it onto the metal. This is a very sturdy and safe type of paint that resists chipping. Make sure that the coating on the bars is non-toxic and won't harm your bird. If you notice that your parakeet is picking away at the coating, *remove the bird from the cage immediately* and get a new cage that does not have a coating. Ingestion of paint or plastic coating can be deadly.

Acrylic cages are expensive, but they eliminate mess. They are

attractive, safe, and save you time on cleaning. Some even come with mechanical ventilation that clears the air inside the cage, a nice feature for allergy sufferers.

Some decorative metal cages have scrollwork that can catch a toe and cause it to break or bleed, which is dangerous for a little bird. Look for simplicity in design and leave the decorative cages to wooden birds. Likewise, wooden pagoda-style cages are unacceptable for parakeets because they can easily chew their way out of them. Stick with safe metals and plastics.

Look for a cage with a door that opens on one side with hinges, like the door to a house, or one that opens from the top and pulls down.

Guillotine-style doors are popular in the less expensive cages, but they are dangerous because they can snap down on a parakeet's head or neck. If you already have a cage with guillotine-style doors, buy some stainless steel quick links online or from your hardware store and keep those doors locked shut. Spring clips will work as well, but if your bird is determined enough, he can move the spring mechanism with his beak and get caught in it.

Where to Place the Cage

Once you've gotten a cage, locate it in your home in a spot that gets some traffic, an area that maintains a sense of relative calm but is well-attended by family members. For example, the living room, family room, and TV room are all good choices, but a hallway is not. Don't put the bird in a room that won't get enough traffic, like a child's room, bedroom, den, or back room, because your parakeet needs a lot of attention and is likely to feel he's missing his "flock" if relegated to an out-of-the-way place. Avoid placing him in rooms that may have fumes or temperature changes, like the bathroom, kitchen, or garage.

Once you've decided on a location, choose a corner of the room to place the cage in. Ideally, it should be near a window, but not against it. Activities outside may frighten the bird, so he should have a safe spot in the cage

Safety vs. Design

The best materials for a parakeet cage are safe metals and hard plastics. Wooden and antique cages can be dangerous because they are easily destroyed and may harbor bacteria or contain toxins. Buy a cage that will be comfortable for your bird, rather than one that appeals to you because of its design or because it suits your décor.

near the wall to retreat to—there may be animals outside that scare him, passing cars, or other disturbances. Don't hang the cage in the middle of the room, or place it out in the open. It should be against at least one wall for the bird to feel secure. Make sure that the spot isn't drafty and doesn't get too much direct sunlight.

The cage should be high enough so that the family cat or dog can't easily get to it. Birds prefer high locations and will feel very insecure on the ground. Parakeets are ground feeders in the wild, so they are programmed to look out for danger when they're near or at ground level. You don't want your parakeet to live in a constant state of fear. He will have a better vantage point the higher he is, which will make him feel safer and happier.

Cage Alternatives

It's absurd to call any bird a "cage bird," but that's still how companion birds are labeled today. They aren't meant to be in cages, a topic often missed in discussions about bird keeping. There's little consideration about what birds need to do most—fly. An aviary is a large cage that offers ample room for flight and can house several pairs of parakeets. You can order a small aviary online or buy one from a bird shop. Ideally, it should be large enough to fit a human adult inside of it comfortably.

A habitat is an aviary taken to the next level. It is larger and contains natural elements, such as plants and running water. Some zoos have habitats, and they are becoming popular with bird fanciers as well. The idea is to recreate, as closely as possible, the animal's natural environment. It would be quite difficult to recreate the Australian grasslands where your parakeet's cousins live, but allowing your birds to fly and interact with the sun and the weather is a start. Since most are built outdoors, there are considerations such as predators and foul weather to contend with, but a well-built and well-planned habitat can withstand such odds.

Place your cage in a warm, sunny, draft-free place where your bird can feel like part of the family.

Bird-Proofing

If your bird is going to spend any time outside of his cage, you will need to carefully bird-proof your home. Here's a list of things to cover:

Windows
Make sure that all windows have screens that don't have any holes in them.

Standing water
Cover all standing water, including fish tanks, dog bowls, toilets, pools, fountains, sinks, and pots in the kitchen.

Electrical cords
Wrap up all cords and hide them.

Fumes
Eliminate nonstick cookware from your home (the fumes from heated nonstick cookware can kill birds); eliminate aerosol cans, scented candles, and all air fresheners.

Smoke
Ban smoking in your home. Nicotine residue builds up on feathers and can cause health disorders.

Household cleaners
Put away all cleaners, fertilizers, jewelry cleaners, paints, and glues.

Lead
Move stained glass away from the bird's area and put away all fishing supplies.

Ceiling fans
Remove fans or put tape over the switch that turns them on.

Fly paper
Don't use it.

Halogen lamps
These become very hot and can burn and kill a parakeet that lands on one.

Laundry and bedding
Always make sure that your parakeet is accounted for before doing a load of laundry. Birds can get into the washer, dryer, laundry basket, or in-between blankets and sheets.

Appropriate cage accessories are essential to your bird's health and well-being.

Furnishings and Accessories

Now that you have selected an appropriate cage, you need to furnish your parakeet's new home. There are, or course, the essentials—cups, bowls, perches, etc.—but there are some wonderful accessories that can add greatly to your pet's quality of life.

Cups and Bowls

The cage you purchased probably came with a couple of cups for seed and water, which are the basics, but you'll need a few more to complete your set. The ones that came with your cage are most likely plastic, which is not the finest material for a coop cup. Plastic can become scratched and harbor bacteria in the grooves no matter how well you clean. Stainless

steel is a great material for bird cups. It's durable, easy to clean, and might even outlast your bird. Ceramic cups are also a good choice, but the surface can become cracked and crazed, and the cup will need to be replaced eventually. Both of these types can be purchased with holders that keep them securely attached to the cage bars.

Ideally, you will have two complete sets of dishes: two for seed/pellets, two for water, and two for fresh foods. Each day you can remove the dirty dishes and replace them with the clean ones, allowing you to then disinfect and dry them for the next day. Cleaning stainless steel cups is easy. Wash them in warm soapy water, making sure to wipe every surface with a textured sponge, and then rinse well. Once a

In order to provide food and water in clean receptacles each day, you should have two sets of dishes.

use water bottles. This is risky because the metal tube can lose suction, leaving your bird without water. Also, bacteria grow rapidly inside the metal tube if it's not cleaned properly. Some people advocate the water bottles because bacteria actually grow slower inside the glass bottle; however, you still have to change the water twice a day, as you would with regular coop cups.

week, soak the dishes for 10 minutes or so in a 10 percent bleach solution (90 percent water) to thoroughly disinfect them.

Tube-style waterers are popular among parakeet owners because the water often stays cleaner longer—there is less area for the parakeet to toss food and droppings into. However, just because the water lasts longer, doesn't mean that you don't have to change it every day. You also have to disinfect it more often because most tube waterers are made of plastic. Some people

The Expert Knows

Parakeet Pastimes

Like most people, you have to come up with ways to keep your parakeet entertained while you're gone. Leave the television or the radio on for your bird. A silent environment is stressful for birds as silence in the wild means that there's a predator nearby. If you can have two or more parakeets, they can "talk" to each other—even if they aren't in the same cage. Toys are the ultimate entertainment, so be sure to offer several types and rotate them in and out of the cage weekly. Finally, food is very entertaining, so offer a wide variety, especially ones that the bird can play with, like greens woven in-between the bars of the cage, corn on the cob, and air popped popcorn.

Beware of tube-style feeders. Because parakeets hull their seeds rather than eat them whole, it may look like they are getting plenty of seed when in reality they only have access to the empty hulls. Add fresh seed to the entire tube every day.

If you're feeding egg, which parakeets do enjoy, you can buy a special plastic egg cup shaped like half an egg that clips on to the side of the cage. Just hard boil an egg, cut it in half, and sit one half inside the cup.

Toys

Toys are essential to the health and well-being of a single parakeet. A pair of parakeets can get along fairly well without them, but there's no reason why they shouldn't have them. Toys keep your budgie occupied; they give him something to do with an otherwise dull daily life inside a cage. Wild parakeets work all day at finding food and water and at staying safe. Your budgie doesn't get nearly this much exercise, though he does require it. Toys are for

Parakeet toys should be colorful, safe, and designed to keep your bird interested and entertained.

chewing, flinging, preening, and carrying out elaborate arguments. A beloved toy can offer a lonely budgie a sense of comfort and a feeling of security and home.

Parakeets love shiny, interactive toys that they can fling around or slather with affection. Some toys are directed toward alleviating loneliness, such as mirror toys, floss and preening toys, and toys shaped like another life-sized budgie.

Though mirror toys are fun and

Toy Safety

Not all toys are safe for your parakeet. Remember, he has a very tiny head that can get caught in a small ring, or he could catch his delicate toes in odd places like the slots in a bell. Old toys with sharp edges or corners, frayed ropes, or loose strings can be hazardous, as well. Be sure to quickly replace any items that become worn or broken.

interactive, your parakeet may become so enamored with his reflection that he becomes obsessed with it. If you notice that your bird is becoming extremely affectionate with his mirror, you might want to remove it temporarily until the bird's affections return to you. However, if the bird doesn't come out of his cage and he gets a lot of joy from playing with the mirror toy, there's nothing wrong with leaving it in his cage permanently.

Parakeets are destructive, but they are not incredibly powerful, which is why there are many plastic toys on the market geared toward them:

- **Wooden toys:** Parakeets love to chew, and toys made from soft wood are perfect for that.
- **Lava and rawhide:** These materials are often included with wooden or plastic toys strung on chain. Both offer the parakeet a way to keep his beak trim.
- **Rope:** Rope toys are fun to preen and chew, but be sure to trim any loose strings that can get caught around a neck or a foot.
- **Plastic toys:** Many parakeet toys are made from plastic, which is an acceptable material for these birds because they aren't strong enough to break it.
- **Acrylic toys:** These toys are more expensive, but many are fanciful and inventive, well worth the cost.
- **Swings:** Parakeets love swings, so offer at least one or two. Swings with innovative perches or toys attached are particularly useful.
- **Spooling toys:** Some toys include a place to add a roll of calculator paper or toilet paper so that your bird can unravel it and chew to his heart's content.
- **Activity centers:** These are all-in-one stations that have a lot of different activities, like rotating wheels or beads on a wire.
- **Foot toys:** These are stand-alone toys (not attached anywhere on the cage) that your parakeet can toss around, for example, cylindrical toys with plastic beads inside.

31

• Dispensing toys: These toys are containers that dispense anything you add, for example, sunflower seeds. The bird has to work to figure out how to get the seeds out.

Rotating the toys in and out of the cage on a weekly basis is a good way to keep the parakeet interested. Removing and replacing them with others also gives you an opportunity to disinfect old toys and refresh any parts that may have frayed or broken. You will need to have an abundance of them on hand to rotate, but be sure to leave the one or two toys that the bird loves inside the cage at all times.

Not all toys sold in the pet shop are safe for your parakeet. Remember, he has a very tiny head that can get caught in a ring, or he can catch his toes in little places, such as the slots in a jingle bell. Old toys with sharp corners or fraying rope can be dangerous as well. File sharp corners with a nail file and trim any loose strings that could potentially get wrapped around a neck or a foot.

Perches of varying widths will exercise your parakeet's feet and also help keep his toenails and beak trimmed.

Perches

The cage you purchased will likely have come with a few plastic perches or a couple of wooden dowels, and though those are fine perches to use, it's an inadequate selection. Because your parakeet uses his feet twenty-four hours a day, it's important that he have as many different perch widths, materials, and textures to stand on as possible. If your bird only has one type and size of perch to stand on, he can develop serious

Homemade Toys

Homemade bird toys are usually inventive and interesting and can be fun to make for your budgie buddy. Here are a few easy ones to try:

• For a nutritious toy, wrap millet inside of white tissue paper and tie it at the ends with a small length of sisal twine. Hang it or place it in the cage. You might have to tear the paper a little the first time to show the bird what's inside.

• For a portable swing, wrap a wooden clothes hanger (one with a pants bar at the bottom) all over with sisal twine. Using lengths of twine, tie plastic buttons, scrunched up tissue paper, and pieces of millet spray to it. You can hang it anywhere you want your parakeet to hang out with you.

• For an activity box/bowl, use a shallow dish filled with different sized marbles, blue berries, cranberries, and air popped popcorn; the bird can move all of the pieces around the dish, and get a treat when he happens upon something edible.

Perches of varying widths will exercise your parakeet's feet and also help keep his toenails and beak trimmed.

foot problems. Think of good perches like orthopedic shoes. Choose hard wooden perches with natural bends and twists and variations in diameter.

You can use perches from your trees outside, but you must be absolutely certain that the type of tree is nontoxic and that it was never sprayed with insecticide. Though your parakeet will enjoy chewing on this "green" wood, he shouldn't be exposed to toxins.

If you use rope perches, be careful to trim all loose strands and make sure that the rope doesn't unravel. Loose strands can wind around a toe or foot and cause injury, and unraveled rope can create an area for the bird to insert his head and potentially get stuck.

Concrete and sand perches are available in all sorts of colors and diameters and can often become a bird's favorite perch, especially for sleeping. This is a rough perch that acts as a nail and beak trimmer. Every parakeet should have at least one of these perches, but not to the exclusion of other types. Many people are fond of those sandpaper sheaths that slip over existing perches. These can become soiled and damp and may allow bacteria to grow that can be harmful to your bird's feet. Toss the sandpaper and use sand perches instead—they are easier to clean.

Electric warming perches are becoming popular now, especially for companion birds that live in colder climates. These plastic perches plug into the wall socket and emit a

Out-of-Cage Playtime

Birds will benefit from having a place to play, get much needed activity, and interact with you all at the same time. Along with providing much needed out-of-cage playtime, a play gym is also a great taming tool because you can work with your bird on a perch away from his cage. Good ones offer the same qualities as a well-designed cage in that they are sturdy and easily cleaned. You can purchase one or easily make your own.

low-grade heat. Birds absolutely love them.

Place perches well away from food or water dishes, not over them. This will help keep the dishes free of droppings (which will wind up in the water no matter what you do!). Don't place so many perches in the cage that your parakeet can't move around. Leave him some space for exercise.

Cuttlebones/Mineral Blocks

The cuttlebone is a standard item in most parakeets' housing. It is actually the central bone of a type of squid. The cuttlebone provides calcium and other essential minerals, as well as providing the parakeet with another fun chewing activity.

A mineral block and a beak block are essentially the same thing—a lump of minerals shaped into a block or another fun shape. Your parakeet will appreciate this treat, and it will help to keep his beak trim, as well as adding some calcium and minerals to his diet.

Active and energetic, parakeets love swings, ladders, and other objects they can climb.

Play Gyms

A play gym, or jungle gym, consists of a platform affixed with perches, ladders, and toys. This will give your bird an opportunity to play and get some much needed activity. A play gym is also a great taming tool because you can place the bird on the steady perch and work with him there, rather than trying to work with him close to his cage, where he might seek refuge.

These gyms can get rather elaborate and expensive, but you can make one yourself out of a clay pot, some plaster of Paris, and some wooden dowels. Plug up the clay pot and fill it with plaster of Paris. Insert wooden dowels of various heights vertically into the plaster. Let the plaster dry, and then tie thinner dowels horizontally to the vertical dowels using sisal twine. Then, tie wooden rings, natural paper cups, and plastic buttons all over the horizontal dowels at different levels. Voila! An easy, homemade play gym.

Lighting

Invest in bird lamps if you live in a part of the country that gets cold and dark for a good portion of the year. You can get special wide-spectrum light bulbs that mimic the sun's rays. Parakeets synthesize vitamin D by spreading oil from a gland on their rump (the uropygial gland) onto their feathers during preening. When the sun's rays hit this oil, it turns into a useable form of Vitamin D, which the bird ingests during preening. If sunlight or a wide-spectrum bulb doesn't hit the feathers, he will not make this important vitamin and may become deficient in it.

Buy a standard, cheap spot lamp from the hardware store and shine it a few feet away from your parakeet's cage. If you can't find bird-specific bulbs, use bulbs made for reptiles— they are very similar. Ideally, the light from the lamp should come from above, so invest in a hanging fluorescent lamp fixture if you can.

Tucked In

Although some birds become frightened in the dark, others like to be covered at night. An appropriate cover can help eliminate nighttime drafts and will allow your parakeet to sleep longer in the morning. In the wild, birds need 10 to 12 hours of shuteye a day and should get about the same amount in the home.

Bedding

The best thing to put into the birdcage tray is plain old newspaper. There's some evidence to show that the ink in the paper actually has antibacterial properties. Your cage should have a grate to prevent your bird from getting to the soiled paper. If it doesn't, consider getting another cage. Other types of bedding are not recommended for birds, including corn cob bedding, walnut shells, newspaper pellets, and wood shavings. These items aren't bad for the birds, but they do hold moisture and can allow bacteria and fungus to grow much faster than newspaper. It's easier to see when newspaper is dirty, and much harder to see the filth with other kinds of bedding. Also, if you ever need to take your bird to the veterinarian because you think he's ill, you can easily show him the droppings on the paper—not so with the other bedding. Plus, used newspaper is free!

Seed Catchers

Some cages come with skirts that catch a good deal of fallen food and waste. If your cage doesn't have one, you can buy a cage "bloomer," acrylic panels, or other plastic guards. These items do work to keep much of the mess inside the cage, but they're not perfect. You will still need to do some floor cleaning.

Black-and-white newspaper is the best bedding and makes daily cage cleaning easy.

parakeet's cage needs regular cleaning and maintenance in order to keep your bird ...hy. Here's a sample cleaning schedule:

...ning Schedule

Daily: Change paper in the tray; wash dishes with warm, soapy water, and rinse well.

Weekly: Remove perches and scrub them in warm, soapy water, then rinse and dry well. Remove the bottom grate and tray and wash well, removing all debris. Remove all toys and check them for broken parts or unraveled rope, then wash and dry them.

Monthly: Dismantle the cage if you can and wash it with soapy water, or place the whole thing in the bathtub or take it outside. Soak in a 10 per cent bleach solution if it's very crusty.

...ning Supplies

Many household cleansers are deadly to your bird, so don't use any chemicals in or around his cage. Instead, use natural disinfectants such as vinegar for cleaning and baking soda for scrubbing. You can use a 10 percent bleach solution for soaking components of the cage, but make sure to rinse very carefully. Grapefruit seed extract also makes a great disinfectant, and you only need 32 drops per quart and a cheap spray bottle. This extract is safe to ingest and can be used all over the house.

Youngsters and Bird Care

No matter how much a child promises that he or she will take care of a pet *no matter what,* it's critical that an adult in the household be the pet's primary caretaker, allowing the child the privilege of supervised care. Watch to make sure that the child is feeding his pet bird every day and changing the paper. You will have to take over more in-depth cage cleaning chores. Remember, a 10 year old might be 24 by the time the parakeet departs for greater pastures. A parakeet is likely to get lost in the shuffle.

38

Parakeets

Cage Covers

If your bird's chirping bothers you early in the morning, consider getting a cage cover. Many companies make them for standard cage sizes, or you can have one custom-made. You can also toss a dark sheet or piece of fabric over the cage as well. Keep an eye out for any fraying or holes in the cover. Your bird can pull at part of the cover or at hanging threads from inside the cage and potentially strangle himself with them.

Grooming Supplies

Bathing is good for your parakeet's skin and is a natural behavior that should be encouraged. Most birds will bathe in their water dish. You can provide your parakeet with a separate bath that he may prefer. A shallow saucer filled with warm water often does the trick. You don't need to use commercially prepared spray baths—these may contain elements that can irritate your bird's eyes. It's probably best to stick with plain tap water.

If you're going to be trimming your parakeet's nails and wings yourself, you will need the correct type of clippers and scissors. (Please see Chapter 4 for more details on these essential items.)

Although it can get messy, bathing is a natural behavior for birds and should be encouraged.

Bird Spa

Putting a special suction-cupped perch on your shower wall is a great way to spend more time with your parakeet and gives him a steamy spa treatment that's great for his feathers and skin. Be careful, however, to prevent him from getting burned by keeping the water temperature on the cooler side in case he inadvertently flies into the stream. Also, close the toilet lid, and never leave him unattended. Put him back into his cage if you're going to use a blow dryer or flat iron, as both may contain nonstick elements that can cause noxious fumes.

look like a round tin with holes punched on one side. This product contains an insecticide that can be harmful for your bird. Even though parakeets can get mites, it's unlikely they will. Mite protectors are not a substitute for good care and veterinary attention. Cloth huts and stuffed toys are popular these days, but they have been known to cause many deaths by choking and crop impaction.

Travel Carriers

Even if you don't plan on taking trips with your parakeet, you will need a travel carrier in case of emergencies. Small bird carriers typically have a door on the top for easy access. They should be easy to clean and small enough to fit beneath the seat of an airplane. They should also have adequate ventilation and a place to put food and water dishes.

Buyer Beware

There are a few popular products on the market that can actually be harmful or deadly for your parakeet. Spiral millet holders pose a hanging hazard, so steer clear of them. Mite protectors are another risky product. These

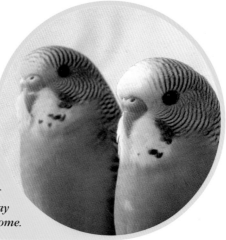

Consider keeping more than one parakeet if you will be spending most of the day away from home.

Chapter 3

Good Eating

"Avian nutrition" is a popular buzz-phrase these days, and for good reason. Food is much more than a basic need. No animal can thrive without quality food and proper nutrition. In the past, bird food was largely designed with convenience in mind, not nutrition and longevity. It was easy to open a bag of seed and just pour it in a dish. Fortunately, bird food manufacturers and avian experts have come a long way in their thinking and research on the topic, and companion birds have reaped the benefits. Sure, seed is still part of the general parakeet diet, but it's only part of the story when it comes to optimal nutrition.

Providing your parakeet with proper nutrition right from the start will help keep him in top shape.

Proper Nutrition

Your parakeet needs many of the same nutrients that you need to be healthy. Here are just three of the many important vitamins and minerals that your bird requires:

Calcium—Calcium is necessary for bones and body function; lack of calcium can cause seizures; deficiency can also cause egg binding in females. For birds, it is available in fortified products, kale, mustard greens and other greens, and almonds. It can also be supplemented in the diet by offering cuttlebone and mineral blocks.

Vitamin A—Vitamin A is the most essential vitamin for birds, it promotes respiratory and liver health. For birds, it is available in leafy greens and orange vegetables. Do not supplement vitamin A without a veterinarian's supervision, as too much can be toxic.

Vitamin C—Vitamin C is necessary for the immune system. For birds, it is available in kale, red peppers, strawberries, and oranges.

As you can see, birds are much like us in their dietary needs. And, like us, the bottom line for their nutritional health is variety. The more food items you feed, the more likely that your bird will eat something healthy. Don't give up on a bird that seems finicky. He will eat what you're offering if you keep offering it. His curiosity will hopefully get the best of him.

Variety

Birds are like humans in their dietary needs and require the same nutrients to be healthy. The key to their optimum health is variety. Be sure to feed a well-balanced diet of seed, fresh vegetables and fruits, grains, and supplements.

What Wild Parakeets Eat

The wild parakeet in Australia consumes seeds from nearly forty types of grass plants. He eats both mature seeds and green seeds and is known to be a nuisance to grain farmers. Though he does eat other types of vegetation, his diet is primarily seed-based. As you will find out in this chapter, seeds do not offer complete nutrition for companion parakeets.

So, how does the wild parakeet survive? He has an important advantage over your house parakeet: lots of exercise. Wild parakeets fly all

day long looking for food and water, both of which can be scarce at certain times of year in their native habitat. They have been recorded traveling over 60 miles (96.6 km) in search of feeding grounds. These wild birds are genetically programmed toward this kind of strenuous exercise. It's likely that your bird isn't getting this kind of workout. Even if he lives in a large aviary, it's impossible to mirror the environment of the wild parakeet. Nevertheless, well-cared-for companion parakeets can live longer than their wild counterparts.

Bird Seed

Companion parakeets can thrive on a seed-based diet, but they can't live on seeds alone. An all-seed diet will cause

Your parakeet requires many of the same nutrients that you do to maintain good health and ensure longevity.

Not only is an all-seed diet unhealthy, it would barely sustain your bird. Be sure to feed him a well-balanced diet.

your parakeet to develop serious health issues and will shorten his life span by well more than half. As odd as it sounds, birds do get fat. An obese parakeet will eventually have health problems, including fatty tumors. These tumors can ulcerate and require surgery, if your bird doesn't die first. Parakeets are also prone to fatty liver disease and iodine deficiency, both due to an inadequate diet.

Seeds are not a bad food, but they are often misused. Many veterinarians suggest that people take their birds off of seeds because they feel that owners may not be responsible enough to provide a varied and healthful diet for their pets. Seeds provide a lot of carbohydrate and fat to your bird's regimen, things that a wild parakeet needs far more than the companion parakeet does. They are certainly easy,

but putting a little extra effort into what you feed your bird will save you upset and veterinary bills in the future. It's worth the time.

Offer seed in small amounts, but certainly not as a total diet. It can make up 20-30 percent of your parakeet's food. Your veterinarian may suggest that you don't feed seed at all, but that choice is yours. Your bird will certainly like it, and it does provide some essential nutritional components.

Choosing the right kind of seed isn't difficult—you'll likely find a bag of seed with a parakeet's image printed right on it. Most mixes contain primarily millet, with some oat groats, safflower seeds, canary seeds, buckwheat, rape seed, flax seed, and others mixed in. If you've got a feed store nearby, you can create your own mix with the seeds that your parakeet likes the best so that there's less waste. The all-in-one mixes don't suit every bird.

Some of the seed mixes found in pet stores are brightly colored and claim to be "fortified" with vitamins. The vitamins are in the coloring that the manufacturer coats the outside of the seed with. The inside, the only part that your parakeet actually eats, remains uncoated. Save your money and buy the plain looking seed at a feed store and spend the difference on healthy fruits and vegetables for your bird. The regular seed is not as colorful, but it's less expensive and will suit your parakeet just fine.

Seeds that have been sprouted are much higher in nutrition than dry seeds, so if you have some time you can make your bird's favorite "junk food" into something very healthy that you can serve in large amounts every day.

Remember in elementary school when you sprouted dry beans in a jar? Sprouting seed is that easy. You can buy sprouted beans at the supermarket, or you can sprout seeds and beans on your own using a sprouting kit from any health food store. Some companies sell a sprouting kit for birds that you can use right out of the box.

You don't need a green thumb to follow these simple steps:

- Rinse the seeds and soak them overnight in cool, clean water.
- Line the bottom of a shallow, flat dish with wet paper towels and spread the seeds in a single layer on top of them.
- Cover the dish with plastic wrap and punch several holes in it.
- Place the pan somewhere warm where it will receive light.

Feeding Tips

Parakeets eat all day and their fast metabolism requires food to be available at all times. So, unlike dogs and cats, you will not remove food from your bird's housing once you feed him. Offer the healthiest foods in the morning when he's hungry. For example, make a fruit and veggie salad in one bowl, and offer a cooked diet and some table foods in another. In the evening, offer seeds and pellets. This way the bird will have already filled up all day on the good stuff and can have the fun stuff later in the evening. Since you won't remove the dish of seed or pellets, your bird can pick through the remains of that during the day if he doesn't like the other stuff you've served. Remember that parakeets hull their seeds, so what looks like a full dish of seeds might actually be a full dish of husks. Feed your bird fresh foods daily.

- Make sure that the paper towels don't dry out.
- In 3-5 days, when the seeds are sufficiently sprouted, rinse them in cold water and store them in the refrigerator.

Sprouted seeds tend to spoil quickly, so keep an eye on them. Don't offer your parakeet rancid or moldy seed! If you notice an odor coming from the seeds or they feel sticky, toss them out. A good trick is to put a few drops of grapefruit seed extract into the water of your last rinse. You can find it in any health food store or online. This extract is perfectly safe for use with birds (and humans) and is actually healthful. It has antibacterial, antifungal, and antiviral properties. You can even put

Grit for Digestion?

Grit is a popularly sold dietary supplement available in any pet store. There are two types: soluble, like oyster shells and cuttlebone, and insoluble, like silica. It is a common myth that parrots need grit in their diet. Most birds eating a healthy, varied diet will not need any form of grit. Parakeets hull their seeds, meaning they eat what's inside, so they don't need little pebbles inside of their gizzard to help grind their food. However, there is evidence to show that small amounts of grit can aid in digestion. Freely feeding grit is not recommended, however, because too much can cause crop impaction, which can be fatal. Offering small amounts of soluble grit once every few months is acceptable, but not necessary.

a couple of drops of it into your bird's water a few days a week.

Pelleted Foods

Pellets emerged on the avian scene a number of years ago and have become a prominent trend in feeding birds. They are a combination of healthful ingredients that the manufacturer shapes into bits that resemble seeds and other foods that birds

Along with other healthy foods, pellets are nutritious and can comprise 50 percent of your bird's total diet.

find interesting, kind of like the way dog or cat food is made. There are countless brands on the market, each claiming that their product is the best. Though pellets can contain some good stuff, there has been a backlash recently against the feeding of pellets as a total diet. Long-term use of a pellet-only diet has shown results similar to long-term use of an all-seed diet.

As with seeds, pellets are not bad, but they are not the only food you should feed your parakeet. Variety is key. Pellets are a good base diet, but feeding them does not mean that you should exclude other foods, such as fruits and vegetables, table foods, and some seeds. Pellets can comprise 40-50 percent of your parakeet's total diet, with the rest consisting of other healthy foods.

Check the label on the pellets: try only to buy all-natural, preservative-free, organic pellets. Pellets that are brightly colored or smell very fruity have additives that aren't healthful for your bird. You might notice that the seed mix you use has these types of pellets in it. Again, be aware of what your parakeet is actually eating. You may be paying for pellets that your bird isn't consuming, which is a waste of money.

The seed versus pellet debate continues among bird experts. The seed camp will never touch pellets, and

The Expert Knows

Diet Change

If you decide to convert your parakeet from one type of diet to another—for example, from a seed-based diet to a pellet-based diet—consult with your avian veterinarian first. Conversion can be stressful, and your bird should be in prime condition before you make the switch. Although parakeets are not known to be picky eaters, they get used to a steady diet quite readily. As a result, it may be difficult to get them to eat properly if their food regimen is changed.

the pellet camp feels that seed is terrible. Then there are some bird keepers that feed both. Beware of the person who tells you to exclude one over the other. Seeds given in moderation are not going to harm your bird. Pellets can be a great base diet if you also offer other foods. Use your own judgment and the advice of your veterinarian. Remember that parakeets are seed-eaters in the wild and their bodies are built to metabolize it well. If you have decided to convert your parakeet from a seed-based diet to a pellet-based diet, get the go-ahead from your avian veterinarian first. Conversion can be stressful, and your parakeet should be in prime condition before you make the switch.

Good Eating

the pellets before you completely remove seed from his diet. Parakeets can starve to death and can otherwise be severely affected by not eating for as little as a day and a half. Never try to convert breeding birds or sick birds, and never make your parakeet switch cold turkey. Younger parakeets will have an easier time converting than older parakeets, so start early. Some pet stores or breeders wean their birds onto pellets, so be sure to ask about the bird's diet before you bring him home. It's likely that your parakeet has been weaned onto seed.

Pesticides

It's important to remember to thoroughly rinse all produce before offering it to your bird. His body is small and the slightest traces of pesticides could endanger him. Feed organic fruits and veggies if you can.

After your veterinarian approves the switch, mix the pellets with the seed in a 50/50 ratio so that your parakeet gets used to seeing the pellets. Gradually reduce the ratio of seeds to pellets each week, until you're only feeding pellets by the fifth or sixth week. Keep offering lots of other foods at this time as well, especially healthy fruits, vegetables, and cooked foods. Make sure that your parakeet is actually eating

Vegetables and Fruit

Vegetables and fruits are a great way to incorporate important vitamins and

Dark green and orange fruits and vegetables are rich in nutrients like vitamin A, which is essential for your bird's health.

If your parakeet is being fussy about his food, try offering smaller or larger pieces or changing his feeding dishes.

which your parakeet needs to maintain a healthy respiratory system. Vitamin A-deficient birds are prone to respiratory, skin, and liver problems.

Wash all fruit and vegetables thoroughly before serving them to your parakeet. His body is small and can be affected by even the tiniest traces of pesticides. Offer organic produce if you can, so that you have one less thing to worry about.

Fruits and vegetables sour quickly in warm weather, so remove them a few hours after you offer them and replace them with a new batch at this time if it's convenient. Leave these foods with the bird longer in cooler weather, but make sure to remove them in the evening.

minerals into your parakeet's diet, and they make a fun addition to it as well. Most companion parakeets don't have a lot to do all day, so playing with different kinds of food offers a great distraction. Try to feed at least four to six fresh vegetables and fruits a day, more if you can. Eventually, you'll get to know what your parakeet's favorites are and you can keep them on hand.

The best fruits and vegetables for your bird are deep green or orange in color. This type of produce has the most nutrients, especially vitamin A,

Offering the fruits and vegetables is the easy part. Getting your bird interested in eating them is tricky. Try chopping, grating, slicing, or offering the food whole. Clipping greens to the side of the cage is a great way to get your parakeet interested in them. Be patient. Offer new things week after week. Parakeets are curious by nature and will eventually try the new food. Offer a whole carrot or a dish of shredded carrots. Try serving various types of greens in shallow dishes full

Fresh Veggies and Fruits Your Bird Can Eat

Vegetables:

beans (cooked)

broccoli

cabbage greens
(all kinds)

carrots

cauliflower

celery

corn

cucumbers

endive

green beans

green peppers

hot peppers

kale

parsley

peas

potato (cooked)

pumpkin

radicchio

red peppers

spinach

sprouts

tomatoes

turnips

watercress

yams

zucchini

Fruits:

apples

bananas

berries (any kind)

cantaloupe

figs

grapes

honeydew

kiwis

mango

oranges

papayas

peaches

pears

pineapple

plums

pomegranates

tangerines

of water. Some birds will bathe in the greens and then dine on them. Each bird's preferences are different.

If your parakeet is still fussy after a few weeks, perhaps it's because he's afraid of the dish you're using, or he's not happy with the way you're offering the food. Perhaps the food is too big or too small. Change the dishes. Cook the vegetables. You can even bake or cook fresh veggies and fruit into breads, casseroles, and other meals. If you're pressed for time, you can use frozen vegetables and fruits—they aren't as good to use as fresh produce, but if that's all you have time for on a particular day, they are better than nothing. Never used canned veggies, however, because they

Toxic Foods

Although birds can basically eat what we eat, be aware that some foods are toxic to them and can be fatal: salty/sugary/fatty foods, pits and fruit seeds, chocolate, mushrooms, dried beans, avocado, raw onions, alcohol, caffeine, and carbonated beverages.

To provide variety, healthy cooked table foods can be a wonderful addition to your parakeet's diet.

contain too much salt. Also, only feed citrus three days a week.

Cooked Diets

Another good addition to your base diet is a cooked diet, which you can buy commercially or make on your own. These diets contain grains, dehydrated veggies and fruits, and supplements. They are easy to cook and keep in the refrigerator for a week. If you want to make one yourself, soak and cook a few types of beans (kidney, lentil, white, garbanzo, etc.), make three or four types of healthy grains (brown rice, amaranth, barley, red wheat, whole oats, etc.), make a batch of couscous, and lightly sauté some veggies, like kale, carrots, yams, tomatoes, and parsley in olive oil. Mix everything together, and freeze in small baggies for your daily portions. Thaw before serving. If you're using the microwave to thaw, make

Birdy Kabobs

A "birdy kabob" is a great way to get your little feathered friend to eat his greens. Simply thread small bits of vegetable and fruit onto the kabob and hang it in the cage. This gives your parakeet the feeling of having to "work" for his food, which is a natural behavior in the wild.

sure there are no hotspots in the food before you serve it. To get your parakeet used to eating a cooked diet, sprinkle his favorite seeds over the mixture to attract him to the bowl.

Caged birds can suffer from obesity, so avoid overfeeding your parakeet and be sure he gets enough exercise.

If you enjoy baking, you can also make a "birdy bread" simply by adding healthy veggies, pellets, nuts, and other items to commercially prepared corn muffin mix. Only feed this to healthy birds that have no history of yeast infection. This is more of a treat than a base diet, but you can offer it a couple times a week and it freezes well.

Table Foods

Healthy table foods can be a great addition to your parakeet's diet. With very few exceptions, your bird can eat anything and everything that you eat.

Don't worry about spices—birds can eat the hottest of peppers because they have fewer taste receptors on their tongues. A good rule for table foods for birds is that if it's good for you, it's probably good for the bird (with the exception of avocado, chocolate, alcohol, and caffeine, which are toxic to them) and if it's bad for you, it's probably bad for the bird, too. So, though junk food is tasty, the salt and fat can be deadly to your little parakeet.

Eggs offer a lot of nutrients, and parakeets usually love them. Boil eggs for about 30 minutes, cool them, and then crush them, shell and all. Make sure to boil the eggs well, because those eggs came from a chicken that could potentially pass a disease on to your parakeet. If you're a whiz in the kitchen (or even if you're not), you can scramble eggs with some pellets or fresh

53

Clean, fresh water should be available to your parakeet at all times.

chopped veggies. Add some grated soy cheese for some extra protein (a bird's digestion isn't really set up to handle cheese or any dairy products).

Whole wheat and nutty grain bread is a great addition to the diet. Whole wheat crackers are good, too, but be sure that they're unsalted. Unsalted peanut or almond butter spread on the crackers or bread is a healthy treat as well. Whole wheat pasta in various shapes makes a nice meal, especially if you add grated veggies and other grains.

Birds can even eat well-cooked flesh meats, like chicken, beef, and fish, but in moderation. Offer these no more than two times a week. Too much protein isn't ideal for your parakeet's diet, but you can feel free to occasionally share your hamburger.

Fresh Water

It's essential that you provide the best water possible for your bird. Parakeets have very small bodies and the build-up of metals and toxins happens much more quickly than in humans, so try not to use water straight from the tap. It contains chlorine, which can leach important nutrients from your bird's body. Bottled drinking water or filtered water is a much better option.

Change your bird's water no less than twice a day. Dirty water is full of bacteria that are potentially harmful for your bird. Water dishes should be clean enough for you to drink out of them. Soak them in a 10 percent bleach solution (90 percent water) once a week to sterilize them. Be sure to rinse them thoroughly before returning them to your parakeet's cage. Change the water each and every day, even two or three times a day if he tends to toss things into it. Even if you have a tube-style waterer, you must change the water daily, or risk your parakeet becoming ill.

A Sample Diet

Here's an idea of how easy it is to

Healthy Treats

Treats are a fun part of your parakeet's dietary regimen and can add a lot of nutrition as well. A commercially produced seed stick treat is always relished, but don't offer these too often because they can be sugary and may contribute to a weight problem. Parakeets love millet spray, also found in any pet shop, but it doesn't offer a whole lot of nutrition, so offer only a couple a week. Air popped popcorn is a healthful and fun snack. Sprinkle it with a little olive oil and some nutritional yeast to pack it full of nutrition. Cranberries and blueberries placed in a shallow bowl are fun because they roll around and present a little bit of a challenge.

create a wholesome diet for your parakeet:

Choose one day a week in which you'll cook for your bird. Make a commercially prepared or homemade mix of beans, grains, and veggies, and freeze it into seven portions. Freezing does eliminate some of the nutritional value, but you'll make up for that with the fresh foods that you offer.

Example #1:

Thaw one portion of the cooked diet and put it on one side of the bowl. On the other side, grate some carrot, and add sliced apple, berries, and melon. In another dish, place chopped greens, turnips, red cabbage, and other veggies.

The first dish will need to be removed in a few hours, or when you get home from work. The second dish will need to be removed before you go to bed. In the early evening, add 1/8 cup of seeds to your parakeet's seed dish, and a couple of tablespoons of pellets (if you're only offering pellets, just add those, and use seed as a treat three days a week). Add two drops of apple cider vinegar to the bird's water.

Example #2:

Add the thawed cooked diet, along with a whole carrot, half an apple, grated beets, and some pear. In the veggie dish, include other types of greens, green beans, and broccoli. In another dish, offer a smashed hardboiled egg and perhaps some well-cooked chicken. Sprinkle nutritional yeast over everything. Later, add seeds and pellets. Add probiotics to the water.

Example #3:

Use the thawed cooked diet, adding plums, chunked papaya, and half an orange to the dish. For veggies, choose pumpkin, hot peppers, and parsley. Offer a dish of cranberries and air popped popcorn as a treat. Later in the evening, offer a millet spray along with the seeds and pellets. In the water, add two drops of grapefruit seed extract and a good-quality vitamin powder.

55

Good Eating

Example #4:

On a day when you're swamped for time and have even run out of the cooked diet, thaw some frozen veggies, cut an apple in half, smash a hard boiled egg, and toss it all in the dish. On this day, add the seed/pellets at the same time.

As you can see, you can vary the fruits and veggies a lot, but always offer the cooked diet and the base diet every day in the evening, after your bird has had time to consume the better stuff. Table foods can be offered every day, but go easy on the protein packed foods, offering them just two or three times a week.

Dietary Supplements

You may have seen water-soluble vitamin or mineral supplements in the bird section of your local pet shop. These companion-grade supplements will probably not harm your bird, but shouldn't really be necessary if you provide a healthy, balanced diet. Before you consider offering them, try to get your parakeet to eat fruits and vegetables that are rich in vitamins, especially vitamin A. These include carrots, sweet potatoes, kale, spinach, butternut squash, mangoes, red peppers, and turnip greens. You can supplement moist foods by sprinkling

If you feed the correct diet, your parakeet should not require supplementation.

in just a few hours, especially in warm weather. If you do decide to occasionally add vitamins to your parakeet's water, be sure that you change it frequently. Most veterinarians are opposed to water supplements for birds, but many keepers do find a good-quality one useful a couple of days a week. Many

With a few exceptions, your parakeet can eat the same healthy foods that you eat.

spirulina or greenfood powder over it. Probiotics, like acidophilus, are great to help balance the bird's digestive and immune system and can be offered in water a few days a week or sprinkled over moist foods.

Supplements meant to be used in water can turn it into a bacteria soup also add one or two drops of apple cider vinegar to the water daily; the acidity in it wards off bacteria and is healthful for your bird. Finally, a couple of drops of grapefruit seed extract in the water a few days a week helps to ward off viruses, fungi, and bacteria.

Chapter 4

Looking Good

Grooming your parakeet is an important part of bird ownership. Birds need to have clean and well-maintained feathers to look and feel their best. Your parakeet will groom himself as a matter of routine during his daily activities. He will preen himself by running his beak through his feathers to make sure they are orderly and clean.

eathers are made up of the rachis, or shafts, onto which smaller strands, or barbs, are attached. The barbs are lined with even smaller strands, the barbules, which are lined with little hooklets. The hooklets and the barbules act like Velcro to stick the barbs together (though the fluffy, white, down feathers near the bird's skin don't have these features). Once stuck together, the feathers look smooth and cohesive. Feathers are delicate, but when they work together, they are strong enough to challenge gravity and give the bird flight.

Feathers also help to insulate the bird against the cold by keeping warm air close to the skin. If they become dirty or the bird gets into something sticky or oily, his ability to regulate his temperature can become compromised. You can see why it's so important for birds to keep their feathers in prime condition. Interestingly, they are

made mostly of a protein called keratin, the same substance as your fingernails. For a bird to have optimum feather quality, he must have an optimum diet.

The parakeet has a gland at the base of his tail at the top of the rump called the uropygial gland, which secretes an oil he gathers with his beak during preening and spreads throughout his feathers. This oil keeps them supple and water-resistant. It also contains elements that are the precursors to vitamin D—when sunlight hits the oil on the feathers, it creates vitamin D, which the bird then consumes as he preens. Isn't nature amazing? This gland can become infected and diseased, largely due to the

Grooming is a normal part of your parakeet's daily routine.

Feather Loss

Molting is a bird's way of replacing feathers that are worn out. The bird will systematically lose feathers from all over his body, but not all at once, and not in patches—bald patches are a sign of illness or a behavioral problem. You will notice more feathers on the bottom of the cage than usual and will see pinfeathers emerging from between the other feathers. Molts occur once or twice a year and can last a few months. Offer your bird a nutritious diet at this time to help with feather production, and include some extra protein.

lack of a good diet—another reason why it's important to feed your parakeet correctly.

Bathing

Parakeets need to bathe to keep their feathers clean and their skin moist. Most will happily bathe themselves and won't need help from you, aside from being given a shallow dish filled with clean water in which to bathe. If the drinking dish is large enough, he will try to bathe in it, which is fine, but you should also offer a separate bathing dish a couple of times a week, perhaps even more often. The dish should be shallow and not easy to tip over. Fill it with about an inch (2.5 cm) of tepid water. Birds prefer to bathe in cooler water, unlike humans.

You might not think that bathing in winter is a good idea, but your home may be too dry from home heating, and the bird will need to keep his skin moisturized. Dry skin can lead to itching and feather chewing, so be sure to provide plenty of opportunity for bathing. Remove the bowl in the evening and dry the cage and surrounding area thoroughly.

Clean, fresh water makes the best bath. You can buy spray bath items from the pet store, but they are not necessary, and some can even irritate the bird's eyes or nasal passages. Some people occasionally add a few drops of glycerin to the water to make the bird shiny, but that's not necessary either.

Some parakeets like being misted or sprayed from above, which is easy enough using an inexpensive spray bottle. Try to mist so that the water falls down like rain, rather than spraying directly at the bird. Some parakeets don't like this method, so don't force it. You'll know if your bird likes it when he rubs his head behind him, opens his wings, preens, and makes other bath time motions. If you mist while he's still in the cage, remove his food dish and the paper beneath the tray and then replace them when you're done.

Bathing in the bathroom shower is great for a very tame bird. Get a suction-cup shower perch and place it above the water stream so that he can get to it if he wants, or move away from it at any time. Then, take your shower as usual (but don't make the water too warm). You can also put the perch high above the shower, and take a steamy shower—the moisture from the steam is great for the bird's skin. However, make sure the bird doesn't jump into the water stream, and if he does, be ready to grab him immediately. Also, when he's in the bathroom, close the toilet lid and make sure that all toxic substances are put away. Remove anything from shelves that he could knock over in case he panics or flies.

Another fun place for a tame parakeet to bathe is the kitchen sink. Remove everything from your clean sink and place a shallow dish at the bottom. Run a small stream of water from the tap into the dish and keep it running. Many birds will run down your arm and right into the sink! You may have to perch your bird on the edge of the dish, but don't force him if he's afraid. Show him the stream of water and encourage him to jump down into the sink. If he's not in the mood, try another day.

Your bird will dry on his own, but you can provide him with a spotlight lamp (ideally with a bird or reptile specific bulb) that will warm him as he preens. There's no need to blow dry your parakeet, especially since some blow dryers have nonstick coating on the heating coils. If you do choose to blow dry and you have a tolerant bird, use a low setting and keep the dryer a few feet from him.

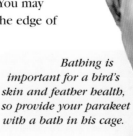

Bathing is important for a bird's skin and feather health, so provide your parakeet with a bath in his cage.

Nail Care

Just like yours, a parakeet's nails grow constantly. In fact, they are made of keratin, just like human nails. If they aren't worn down enough by perching, the nails will get sharp, making any interaction with you unpleasant. Also, if they get too long, the toes will not curl correctly when gripping, which can cause foot problems.

Using concrete or sand perches of many sizes will help keep your bird's nails trim. Some birds will never

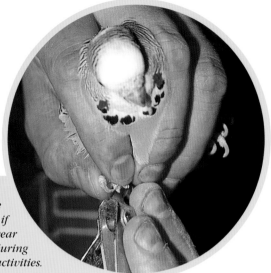

Nail trimming should only be necessary if toenails do not wear down naturally during normal activities.

FAMILY-FRIENDLY TIP

Trimming Tip

If you're not sure of how to hold your bird when trimming his nails, or you're nervous about it, you can use the "sneak up" method. Have the bird perch on one hand, while you talk sweetly to him as a distraction, then sneak up on one toenail with a clipper and carefully snip off the very end. Then you're done for the day. Do this for eight days in a row and you'll clip all of the nails without all the drama.

need their nails cut. If yours does, you may want to consider a trip to the veterinarian or a local bird shop that does grooming. It's very simple to trim the nails yourself, but you have to know how to hold the bird correctly in order not to hurt him.

The nail has two parts, just like human nails: the dead part of the nail (on the end), and the quick, where the blood supply is. Cut the dead part of the nail, never the quick. This is easy when you have a parakeet with light colored nails because you'll be able to see the vein in the nail and avoid it. If you have a bird with dark colored nails, simply trim a very tiny amount off of the tip of the nail rather than risk hurting him.

A human nail trimmer for babies works well for your parakeet's little

nails. A very small cat nail trimmer (guillotine-style) is ideal. Keep styptic powder or cornstarch on hand at all times when trimming in case of bleeding. Simply dip the bird's nail into the powder and then tap it down.

Instead of clipping, you can make a few passes at your parakeet's nails with a file once a week, which will keep them trim and eliminate the chances of hurting your bird. With clipping and filing, less is more—don't over do it.

Beak Care

The parakeet's beak is made of the same material as the nails, keratin, and is built over a honeycomb-like structure that makes it very light. A healthy bird performs activities with his beak that will naturally wear it down, such as

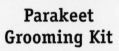

Parakeet Grooming Kit

Grooming supplies for your parakeet include:
- a shallow dish for bathing
- a spray bottle for misting, if your parakeet likes that
- small nail clippers or guillotine-style cat nail clippers
- small, sharp scissors for wing trimming (or scissor-style cat claw trimmers).

eating hard foods, playing with toys, wiping it on perches, and chewing on wood. If your parakeet's beak seems overgrown, he may have a health disorder that needs to be addressed by a veterinarian. Scaly face mites, or *Knemidocoptes* or *Cnemidocoptes*, can infect the beak (and legs), causing it to overgrow. The legs and the cere,

Regularly check your parakeet's beak for any abnormalities; some conditions may indicate a health problem.

Parakeets

the fleshy area over the beak, can be infected with white and gray lesions. Mites are then transmitted from parents to chicks and live their whole life cycle on the bird. They can be transmitted from bird to bird with too close contact. Treatment by a veterinarian is easy and effective.

Malnutrition can also cause the beak to overgrow. It is not advisable to trim your bird's beak because you can severely injure your bird if you don't know what you're doing. If you notice something wrong with it, please visit a veterinarian.

Grooming as a Health Check

When grooming your bird, you should look for any abnormalities. Examine the face and feet. Check the bird's underside and beneath the wings for lumps, bumps, or sores. Feel the keel bone (it runs vertically along his breast), and make sure that the bird isn't too thin—the keel bone should be prominent, but there should be flesh on either side of it. If it is very sharp, the bird is too thin; if you can't feel it at all, he may be too heavy or have a tumor there. If you get your bird groomed by an avian vet, he or she will give him a body check and will be able to detect if something is amiss.

65

Wing Clipping

To prevent a bird from flying, some people trim the lower half of the primary flight feathers (the first ten feathers starting at the outside of the wing) off of both of the wings. This practice is common among companion bird owners and is a painless procedure, much like getting a haircut. Like hair, the flight feathers do grow back, usually in about five to six months, or after a molt. If you want to keep your parakeet's wings clipped, check the flight feathers every month or so to make sure none have grown out.

Wing clipping is a much-heated discussion among bird enthusiasts.

The following are the primary pros and cons:

Safety

Pro clipping—Your parakeet will not be able to fly away and can get lost if you or someone in your household carelessly opens a window or a door, which happens frequently.
Con clipping—A clipped bird has no defense against predators in the home, like the family dog or cat.

Temperament

Pro clipping—A parakeet that has his wings clipped is more manageable and

If you decide to clip your bird's wings, have a professional show you how to do it first.

sweet, more easily tamed and willing to stay tame.

Con clipping—Clipping a parakeet takes away his "birdness." An unclipped parakeet has more self-direction and is able to make choices in his life. He will choose to be with you when he wants, which is better than forcing him to do so.

Flying

Pro clipping— A bird is meant to live in a cage.

Con clipping—A bird is meant to fly.

Home Dangers

Pro clipping—A home is not a safe place for a bird to fly. There are many dangers, including mirrors and closed windows, standing water, and toxic substances that an unclipped bird can find more easily than a clipped bird.

Con clipping—True, a home is not very safe for a bird to have full flight in; therefore, a conscientious owner would build a flight cage or an aviary in which to offer his bird full flight.

Whether or not you clip your bird's wings depends largely on his housing and how you're going to be interacting with him. Many parakeet owners do build aviaries and habitats for their

with you, you shouldn't need to clip him because he will choose your company over sitting on top of the curtain rod. On the other hand, many households, especially those with children, aren't equipped to handle a flighted parakeet because of open windows and doors and other hazards. Only you know what kind of household you have and whether or not your bird is safer clipped or unclipped.

birds. This is a great way to allow your birds to fly and get their necessary exercise. Flying is a wonderful psychological and physical experience for birds and is what they are meant to do. Some believe that taking that away from them is akin to breaking someone's legs so that they can't move very far.

That being said, an untamed parakeet that you intend to tame does need to be clipped during the training process. If not, he's just going to fly away and you won't get any taming done. Once he's tame, if you have a good relationship and he likes being

How Much to Clip

Some owners decide to trim the lower half of their bird's primary flight feathers to prevent them from flying. It's important to keep in mind that clipping should allow your parakeet to flutter gently to the floor. If you cut too much, there is potential for injury from falling. If you cut too little, your bird could fly off into the wild blue yonder. Therefore, it's best to have someone experienced, like an avian veterinarian or breeder, do it for you or teach you how to do it properly.

Not a Kid's Job!

Children should not be responsible for any aspect of grooming a parakeet, but they can certainly help to regularly clean and re-fill the bath dish and put it back inside the cage. They can also be at the veterinarian's office to soothe and calm the bird after nail or wing clipping.

68

Parakeets

Learn to clip your parakeet's wing feathers by watching someone experienced in clipping, like an avian veterinarian, a breeder, or a bird shop owner. You won't have to clip your bird yourself if you can find someone in your area who will charge you just a few dollars. It's worth the effort and the cost not to have to do it yourself.

The wing clip should allow your parakeet to flutter gently to the floor,

not land with a thud. A severe wing clip can cause the bird to panic and not be able to navigate to the floor well. If you cut too little, the bird could still take off into the wild blue yonder.

Clipping a parakeet is a job for two people—one to hold the parakeet in a small hand towel and one to clip the wings. The person clipping extends the wing carefully, holding it at the middle joint (equivalent to the elbow), exposing the individual feathers. You will see the primary flight feathers at the end of the wing, with shorter feathers, the coverts, covering the upper part of the flight—don't cut those shorter

An important part of bird ownership, grooming helps to keep your parakeet happy and safe.

Molting Assistance

Grooming can be stressful for a bird, especially if you have to restrain him. But there's another aspect to grooming that can be pleasant for him – helping to remove feather sheathes. A single parakeet doesn't have another bird to help him at molting time to remove feather sheathes on his head and face. All he can do is scratch at them. If your bird is very tame, have him sit on your shoulder or chest while you gently rub the sheathes between the fingernails of your thumb and forefinger. Not only does this feel good to the bird, it's nice bonding time. If he quarrels or gets agitated, just be gentler with your touch.

feathers! Cut the flight feathers parallel to the coverts, about two millimeters away from them. Parakeets are light and are good flyers, so cut seven to ten of the flights to make sure he can't still fly. For clipping, use a pair of small, sharp scissors or a scissor-style cat claw trimmer, the type with a concave area on both blades. Cut one feather at a time, not all at once.

Never, ever cut into a feather inside a sheath. This is a "living" feather and it will bleed. Blood feathers, also called pin feathers, are newly grown feathers that still have a blood supply. Recognize blood feathers by the sheath of milky white material encasing them. If your parakeet is light in color, you may even be able to see a vein inside the feather. Trim feathers in a clean, well-lighted place, and keep cornstarch

on hand in case you accidentally clip a blood feather (don't use styptic powder because it can burn the skin). Or, you can pull the bleeding feather out firmly but gently from the root; leaving it inside the wing can cause infection. When in doubt, visit your avian vet.

Trim the feathers on both wings evenly. Don't trim only one wing. This does not allow the parakeet to control his descent, and he could easily injure himself trying to land. Some people will advise you to leave the first two primary flight feathers intact, but this is not a recommended practice. Your parakeet could break these feathers easily because the other feathers on the wing no longer protect them—the wing is strong as a cohesive unit, but the feathers themselves are easily breakable.

Chapter 5

Feeling Good

Though parakeets are small birds and their health care might seem relatively straightforward, they are actually very complex organisms. A good guardian should keep an observant eye on the daily health and behavior of his or her feathered companion.

Finding an Avian Veterinarian

An avian veterinarian specializes in the care and treatment of birds. Birds are obviously quite different from dogs and cats and need a special doctor trained in the particular treatment of avian accidents, ailments, and diseases. A veterinarian that does not specialize in birds may not catch a subtle symptom or may not perform the proper tests.

Take your new parakeet to an avian veterinarian within three days of buying him. There are several good reasons for the visit:

- If you bought your parakeet with a health guarantee from a shop, you will have some recourse if tests reveal that your new bird is ill.
- You will begin a relationship with the avian veterinarian who will get to know your bird and be able to

evaluate him better because he or she will have a "healthy reference" for him.

- Some avian veterinarians will not take an emergency patient unless the bird is a regular client.
- Avian veterinarians often board birds in their offices, though some will only board clients.
- You will receive important recommendations from the vet, including information on diet and housing.

The best place to find an avian veterinarian is by calling the Association of Avian Veterinarians at (561) 393-9801 or looking them up on the Internet at www.aav.org. You can also ask the members of your local bird club or society about the ones they use.

Your parakeet should visit an avian veterinarian for checkups at least once a year.

The Vet Visit

After the initial visit, you should take your parakeet to the veterinarian for a yearly "well bird" checkup. Some people do this every six months, which isn't a bad idea. The money that you spend on these health checks will be far less than you have to spend on an emergency visit if you notice that your bird is ill.

The veterinarian will give your bird a physical examination and weigh him. Then the doctor may take cultures from the bird's vent or mouth and take blood for testing. All of these tests show whether or not the bird is in good health, and they are absolutely necessary. Ask your vet which tests are being run and what they will indicate so you can stay informed.

General Signs of Illness

It's critical to be able to recognize the signs of illness in your bird. The first clue that most people get when their bird is ill is a change in attitude, behavior, or routine. There may be changes in the bird's vocalizations, where he stands in the cage, how much he sleeps, the quality of his breathing, and the quality of his tameness. Parakeets, like most birds, appreciate routine, and a sudden break in it signals that you should at least investigate your bird's condition. Perhaps something has frightened him or the temperature has dropped or risen too much. There are possibilities

73

FAMILY-FRIENDLY TIP

Vet Visit Jitters

Going to the doctor isn't fun for anyone, and a child may become concerned about what the veterinarian is going to do with his or her parakeet. Explain that the visit is necessary to keep the bird happy and healthy. At most veterinary visits, the doctor will come into the office to speak with you and your child, but then take the bird into the back to conduct the testing. Prepare the child for this and let him or her know that the bird will come back. Bring some millet spray as a treat that the child can give the bird when the visit is over.

other than illness. If you can't find any reason for your bird's unusual behavior, start looking for the following:

- Fluffiness: If you notice that your parakeet has his feathers fluffed, he is trying to keep heat close to his skin and is having trouble regulating his temperature. Fluffiness might occur in conjunction with sleepiness, sleeping on two feet instead of one, or sleeping on the bottom of the cage.
- Sleeping too much: A parakeet that is

sick may sleep more than usual. Sleeping on the bottom of the cage is especially telling, as is sleeping on two feet instead of one.

- Loss of appetite: You should know how much and what your parakeet is consuming each day. If you notice that your bird is not eating enough or if he stops eating, there is a problem.
- Attitude change: Your parakeet might be ill if he seems listless and is not behaving in his usual manner.
- Lameness: If your bird can't use his feet, you can be guaranteed that there is a problem. Lameness can occur as a result of egg binding, injury, seizure, or other conditions.
- Panting or labored breathing: Either

A change in your parakeet's normal behavior could signal the onset of an illness.

of these symptoms can indicate a respiratory ailment, or perhaps overheating.

- Discharge: If you notice any runniness or discharge from the eyes, nostrils, or vent, take your bird to the veterinarian immediately.
- Food stuck to the feathers around the face: This indicates poor grooming or vomiting, both possible signs of illness.
- Droppings change drastically: Your parakeet's droppings should consist of a solid green portion, white urates (on top of the green), and a clear liquid. If any of these are discolored (darker green, black, yellow, or red) and there has been no change in diet, or you notice undigested food in the droppings, there might be an illness present.

Health Alert

A healthy parakeet is usually active, vocal, and keeps his feathers in good condition. An ill parakeet may not keep up with grooming and "let himself go." He may also look sleepy and listless and spend a lot of time on the bottom of the cage. If you notice anything unusual over an extended period, seek veterinary attention promptly because a bird's condition can decline rapidly.

It's important to know the signs and symptoms of conditions that require a trip to your avian veterinarian.

Parakeet Anatomy: Signs and Symptoms

Here are some more specific points to look for in both a healthy and an ill bird.

Eyes

A bird has one eye on either side of his head, allowing him to see almost 360 degrees around his environment. This helps him to watch for predators and other dangers. Birds also have a second eyelid that acts as a kind of squeegee for the eye, keeping it moist and clean. A healthy eye is clear, moist, and free of discharge. A parakeet with an eye problem may squint or scratch it excessively with his foot, or will rub it on the perch or sides of the cage. Look for swollen eyelids, cloudy eyes, excessive blinking or discharge, and tearing.

Ears

Your parakeet's ears are located a short distance parallel to and behind the eyes and are covered by small feathers. You may get a glimpse of them after your parakeet bathes, when the feathers around the head are wet and stuck together. Birds can't hear in the same range that we do, but they can hear in greater detail. If you can see your parakeet's ear opening without the bird being wet, make an appointment with your avian veterinarian.

Beak

Your parakeet experiences much of his world through his beak and feet. The beak is made of the same durable material as our fingernails and grows over a honeycomb-like structure that is basically hollow, a convenient design for an animal that needs to fly. The beak acts as a crushing tool, but is also delicate enough to peel the skin off a pea. It also functions to help your parakeet around, kind of like another foot. The cere, the fleshy place just above the beak, can sometimes become thick and rough in hens, a condition called brown hypertrophy. This is likely caused by hormones and can be removed by a veterinarian. This is not a serious condition, but should be treated nonetheless.

Feet

Parakeet's feet are zygodactyls, meaning that they have two toes pointing forward and two toes pointing backward. This makes a parakeet very adept at grasping and climbing. Birds use their feet to regulate body temperature. During cold weather, they can decrease the amount of blood circulating to their legs and will often draw one leg up into the body and stand only on the other. When parakeets are warm, they will increase the blood flow to their legs to cool off.

Feathers

Feathers are one of the most amazing, functional parts of a bird, helping him to fly, regulate temperature, and repel water. The parakeet has about 2,000-3,000 feathers on his body. A healthy parakeet should be obsessed with taking care of his feathers, preening them for much of the day.

Birds molt about once or twice a year, usually during seasonal changes

The Expert Knows

Sick Bay

Having a hospital cage on hand is important in case of emergencies and illness. It's a comfortable, warm, safe place for your parakeet to calm down and recuperate. Line a 10 gallon (37.9 l) aquarium with paper towels, and place a heating pad on low to medium underneath one-half of the aquarium—your bird must be able to move away from the heat if he gets too warm. Put a mesh cover on it and drape a towel over three-quarters of the tank. Place a very shallow dish of water (a weak bird can drown in even an inch of water) on one end, as well as some millet spray and seeds or pellets. Do not include toys or perches, but you may include a rolled up hand towel for snuggling. Place the cage in a quiet location and clean the papers once a day or when they become soiled.

when sunlight becomes shorter or longer. Molting is the process by which a bird loses some of the old feathers on his body and grows new ones. When your parakeet molts, you will notice feathers on the bottom of the cage, but you should not be able to see patches of skin on his body. Molting birds might scratch themselves more often as the new feathers break out of their skin. This is not the time to try a new training method. A molting bird will appreciate a bath or spraying offered daily, with some aloe vera juice mixed in with the water.

Occasionally, parakeets that have physical or psychological issues will pick at and chew their feathers. If the cause is medical or nutritional, an avian veterinarian may help solve the problem. If it is psychological, you may have to be more diligent in caring for your bird and keeping him happy. A bird that is confined or kept in stressful situations may pick himself in order to relieve the stress or boredom. Provide your bird with enough space and toys, and, of course, a trip to the veterinarian.

If your parakeet becomes soaked in oil, he will no longer be able to regulate his body temperature, a condition that can be deadly. Dust the oil soaked bird with cornstarch or flour, and then gently bathe him in a small tub of warm water and some mild grease-fighting dish soap. Don't scrub the bird and don't wet his head!

You may have to repeat this process several times. Keep the bird in a warm area until most of the oil is removed and the bird is dry.

Sometimes a wing or tail feather will break in the middle of the growth process and begin to bleed. This is not a serious injury and is one you can deal with yourself. Keep some cornstarch on hand in the case of a bleeding emergency such as this one, and apply the product until the bleeding has stopped. Next, you will need to remove the feather with a pair of needle-nosed pliers. While restraining the bird (you may need two people for this procedure), simply gently grasp the broken feather with the pliers close to the shaft, and pull straight out. This will stop the bleeding and prevent infection. If you are too squeamish to

It is normal for birds to molt, or loose old feathers, once or twice a year.

Only an avian veterinarian should diagnose and treat any health problems your parakeet may have.

cookware, and tobacco smoke. Birds don't breathe in the same way as humans. We inhale and exhale, completing one breath. Birds have to take two breaths for our one. The first breath fills the air sacs, located in hollow spaces in the body and in some of the bones, and the second breath pushes the air into the lungs.

Birds are prone to respiratory illness and distress because their system is more complicated than ours. If you notice your parakeet panting, call your avian veterinarian. Also, always be

do this yourself, take your parakeet to your avian veterinarian.

Respiratory System

Your parakeet has a very sensitive respiratory system that is sensitive to airborne irritants, such as aerosol sprays, fumes from heated nonstick

Toxic Cookware

Nonstick cookware offgasses toxic fumes when overheated, and these fumes are deadly to birds. Birds don't even have to be in the kitchen for the toxicity to overtake them—they can be anywhere in the home. There is no warning sign that birds are about to be overcome; they just drop off their perches—dead. Just before this occurs, they may wheeze and gasp, but by then it's too late to save them. Small birds are especially susceptible. Avoid nonstick pots and pans, drip plates, burner drip pans, cookie sheets, light bulbs, and space heaters, just to name a few.

sure to keep him away from fumes and airborne toxins. You can recognize a respiratory infection by a change in breathing and, in extreme cases, bubbling from the mouth or nostrils. If you notice these symptoms, take your parakeet to the veterinarian right away. An overheated bird will pant and spread his wings trying to cool himself. If this is unsuccessful and the heat does not abate,

Birds have sensitive respiratory systems, so keep them away from fumes and airborne toxins.

the bird may lose consciousness and even die. If you notice that he is becoming overheated, remove him immediately to a cooler place and run a fan near his cage. Lightly mist him with cool water and offer drops of cool water in his mouth. Never set a parakeet out in the sun unless he has a shady spot to retreat to, and never leave a parakeet in a closed car on a warm day because birds are easily overcome by heat.

Musculoskeletal System

Birds are fantastic athletes, able to fly for miles a day, and, as a result, tend to be well-muscled. Parakeets that have their wings clipped are less muscled than fully flighted parakeets. They have more "red" than "white" muscles because they are active flying birds, as opposed to grounded birds, such as chickens and turkeys, who don't need as many fat-burning muscles. Many of your parakeet's bones are filled with air, and all of them are thin-walled, which makes the bird light, a necessary development for flight. A heavy bird expends a lot more energy in the air. While bird bones are strong enough to allow the movement of wings in flight, they are easily broken. If you suspect that one of your parakeet's bones is broken, take him to the veterinarian immediately. Some of the bones contain air sacs that aid in breathing.

Digestive System

The parakeet's digestive system begins with the beak and ends with the vent. After food is swallowed, it goes to the crop, which is near the bird's breast.

Your Parakeet's First Aid Kit

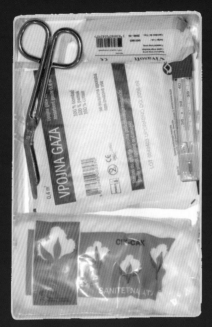

Here is a list of essential items for an avian first aid kit. Keep these items in a small tackle box for convenient access when you need them.

- antibiotic ointment (for small wounds, use a nongreasy product only because oil prevents a bird from keeping in body heat)
- alcohol (for sterilizing tools)
- baby bird formula (can be used for adults having a difficult time eating)
- bag or can of your bird's base diet (in case of evacuation)
- bandages and gauze
- bottled water (you may need clean, fresh water to flush out a wound or clean your bird of debris)
- cornstarch (to stop bleeding on the skin or beak)
- cotton balls
- cotton swabs
- dishwashing detergent (mild, for cleaning oil off of feathers)
- electrolyte solution for human babies (for reviving a weak bird)
- eyewash
- heating pad (always allow your bird the option of moving off of the heating pad)
- hydrogen peroxide (always use in a weak solution with water)
- nail clippers
- nail file
- needle-nosed pliers (for broken blood feathers)
- nongreasy first aid lotion
- penlight
- saline solution
- sanitary wipes
- sharp scissors
- small transport cage
- small, clean towels (for holding or swabbing)
- spray bottle (for misting)
- styptic powder (to stop bleeding on the nails)
- syringe (without needle)
- tweezers
- veterinarian's phone number

Proper husbandry and a healthy diet go a long way in keeping your parakeet in good health.

After going to the crop, the food goes to the stomach (proventriculus), then on to the gizzard (ventriculus), which grinds the food, then on to the cloaca, the place where the feces and urates collect before being eliminated through the vent.

Common Illnesses

Now that you know a little bit about the parakeet's physical body, here are a few diseases and conditions common to this species.

Mites

Scaly-face mites, or *Cnemidocoptes*, occur in young parakeets and older birds with

Attention!

Just like humans, birds can suffer from stress. Parakeets are very intelligent and social creatures, so it's important to provide enough cage space and various toys to keep your bird from feeling bored and restless, especially if you keep only one bird. Also be prepared to devote time to interact and play with your pet each day; out-of-cage time and attention are necessary for his overall well-being. Birds that are confined, lonely, or kept in stressful situations may pick at themselves or develop other behavior problems attempting to relieve discomfort or boredom. You must be diligent not only in providing general care for your parakeet, but making sure he is happy as well.

compromised immune systems. These mites cause a crusty appearance on the bird's face and legs and can result in an overgrown beak. They are easy to treat, but require multiple treatments. Scaly-face mites are not very contagious, but can be passed from bird to bird.

The tiny feather mite is not common in parakeets, but can infest birds that live outdoors in unclean conditions. Red mites eat their host's blood and are highly contagious, though not very common in parakeets. Air sac mites occur more commonly in finches and canaries, but can occur in parakeets and cause a clicking sound when the bird breathes, eventually cutting off the air supply. If you suspect mites, do not try to get rid of them yourself—contact your avian veterinarian.

Giardia

Giardia is a one-celled protozoan that can affect your parakeet, but it can also affect other animals in the house, even yourself. It is passed by contaminated food or water and affects the digestive tract. You may notice diarrhea, itching, inability to digest foods, weight loss, and other symptoms. Have your veterinarian test for this parasite.

Worms

Roundworms are commonly found in parakeets and should be tested for on your first veterinary visit. If roundworms are found, routine tests and treatments should be done on the bird. Eliminating these worms can sometimes take years.

Aspergillosis

Aspergillosis is a fungal infection that causes respiratory distress and can be deadly. Any changes in your parakeet's breathing, changes in vocalization, gasping, or wheezing can indicate this infection. Aspergillosis is diagnosable by your avian veterinarian, but it's difficult to treat, and may take months of medication and treatment to cure.

You can help prevent the common illnesses birds are prone to by keeping your parakeet's cage clean, well-ventilated, and dry.

Quarantine

Quarantine is traditionally a period of forty days in which a new bird is kept separate from other pets already established in the household. Some people choose to shorten this period to thirty days and find little harm in doing that. During the quarantine period, you'll watch the new bird for signs of illness. You should feed and water him after you care for your other birds, and change your clothing and disinfect your hands after any contact with the bird or his cage. Quarantine is the only way to prevent a new bird from passing a potential illness to the birds you already have. It is sometimes not possible to completely separate a new bird from established birds, but you should try to do your best to keep contact at a minimum while he is being quarantined.

Prevent this infection by keeping your parakeet's environment very clean and dry to stop the growth of mold.

Yeast

Yeast infections, or candidasis, affects the mouth, digestive tract, and can involve the respiratory system. Your parakeet normally has a certain amount of yeast in his body, but when his bodily balance is out of whack, like when he's undernourished or after a treatment of antibiotics, the fungus yeast can grow to excess.

A parakeet with a yeast infection will have a sticky substance in his mouth and may have white mouth lesions. Regurgitation and digestive problems may occur. Treatment by a veterinarian is necessary. Even though this condition is not immediately serious, it can cause death if left untreated. Offering your parakeet foods that are loaded with vitamin A, such as green leafy vegetables and orange fruits and vegetables, can help prevent yeast infections.

Tuberculosis

Mycobacterium avium is responsible for the tuberculosis infection in birds and can be transmitted in food, water, or by filthy cage parts. Avian tuberculosis can be transmitted to humans with compromised immune systems, so the caretaker must be careful to avoid infection. While TB in humans is a respiratory disease, it is primarily a digestive disorder in parakeets. Symptoms in birds include weight loss and other digestive disorders.

Psitticosis (Parrot Fever)

Psitticosis, also called chlamydiosis and parrot fever, is transmittable to humans and causes respiratory distress symptoms in both humans and birds. Psitticosis is transmitted through droppings and infected secretions. Some parakeets can be carriers of the disease without showing any symptoms. Ask your veterinarian to test for this disease, especially if there's someone with a weakened immune system, an elderly person, or an infant in contact with your parakeet.

Megabacteria

Megabacteria are large bacterium found in parts of the parakeet's digestive system. They cause extreme weight loss, and diagnosis generally occurs after death. It is not certain whether these bacteria actually cause the condition or whether a weakened system and poor nutrition allow them to thrive.

Psitticine Beak and Feather Disease (PBFD)

PBFD is an incurable, contagious (to other birds) disease that involves feather loss and beak lesions in the later stages of the disease. Diagnosis is through blood testing, and euthanasia is generally recommended after confirmation. This disease is fatal. Symptoms include feather loss, abnormal feather growth, and a generally ill condition.

Polyoma Virus

Polyoma virus usually affects young parakeets, though adult birds are carriers, transmitting the disease to their young, which die around the time they are fledgings. It occurs mainly among breeding stock in crowded conditions, though households with many birds are susceptible as well, especially if you are going to be adding young birds to the household. There is no treatment for polyoma virus, so prevention is essential. Make sure to have your avian veterinarian test all of your parakeets for this disease.

Pacheco's Disease

Pacheco's disease is a viral hepatitis that affects the liver. It is fatal and is mainly diagnosed upon death, which comes rapidly. This is a highly

Treatment should be provided at the first sign of a problem to ensure the best recovery.

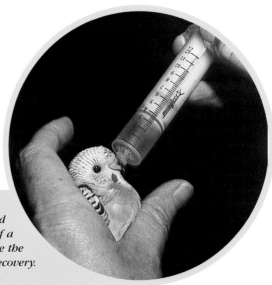

belly is distended and her droppings are large and watery, she may be trying to lay an egg. Give her some time to lay it on her own, but if 24 hours pass and she hasn't laid it, you may need to intervene. If you can't get her to an avian veterinarian right away, place a few drops of olive oil in her vent (just at the outside of it) and a couple of drops in her mouth—be careful that you don't choke her. This may help to lube the area and ease the egg out. If that doesn't work, try it again and move her into a very warm hospital cage and call your avian veterinarian. Even if she passes the

contagious disease and can be transmitted easily when you bring a new bird into your home. Always enforce strict quarantine.

Reproductive Disorders

An undernourished egg-laying hen, especially one that hasn't gotten enough calcium in her diet, may have eggs with soft shells that will be difficult to lay, resulting in egg binding. This can also occur when the egg is malformed, or if she has a tumor or other disorder of the reproductive system. Symptoms of egg binding are panting and lameness, among others. Keeping the laying hen fit and nourished will help to prevent this problem. Consult your veterinarian immediately if you suspect any disorder. If you notice your female bird fluffed on the bottom of her cage, panting, and her

Importance of Exercise

Although healthy parakeets are active birds in general, they can become obese if they are overfed or if they don't get enough exercise. Providing spacious living quarters and providing ample out-of-cage time daily can help to prevent this problem. The best exercise is to let your bird out to play with you. The more exercise your parakeet gets, the healthier and happier he will be.

Poison Control

If your bird comes in contact with poison and you notice evidence of vomiting, paralysis, bleeding from the eyes, nares, mouth, or vent, seizures, or shock and you're not able to get to an avian veterinarian right away, he may have become poisoned. Call the National Animal Poison Control Center's 24-hour Poison Hotline at:
(800) 548-2423
(888) 4-ANIHELP
(900) 680-0000.
If you can, try to discover what your bird has ingested so that they can better help you.

egg, she might need an examination so that the situation doesn't occur again.

Older male parakeets may develop tumors on their testicles (located inside their body), and as a result their cere may change colors. Regular veterinary checkups should help to find and treat any developing problems such as this one.

Gout

Gout is a painful condition of the legs common in parakeets that don't get proper nutrition, including lots of fruits and vegetables. Symptoms include visible swellings on the legs and subsequent lameness.

Bumblefoot

Bumblefoot is an infection of the bottom of the feet and is associated with poor nutrition and obesity. The skin on the bottom of the foot may be inflamed and red and may become scabby, resulting in lameness.

Lameness

Lameness and weakness in the feet are sometimes associated with egg-bound hens, but there can be multiple reasons for it, including tumors. See your avian veterinarian if you notice any foot or leg weakness.

Birds and Bees

The birds and the bees...you can't stop them. But you can prevent your birds from having unwanted babies should they begin mating. First, do not provide them with anything resembling a nest. If they lay eggs in the feed dishes, remove the dishes and replace them with smaller dishes. If they lay eggs on the floor of the cage, simply remove them and throw them away. If the egg laying persists, cut back on the light that your birds get to about 10 hours a day. More than 12 hours of light can cause the birds' hormones to spike, causing them to want to breed.

Senior Bird Care

Because parakeets can live to be fifteen years old or more, they aren't considered "senior" until they are about nine or ten. Unfortunately, because parakeets are inexpensive, they are considered "throw-away pets" and are often not given the proper care, reducing their life span by a third. Most parakeets don't live more than five to seven years in the average home, but you can do better and avoid this tragedy by offering proper nutrition, veterinary care, a parakeet-proofed home, and spacious housing.

A very elderly bird might have trouble getting around and may need his perches lowered and his food served on the floor of his cage. He might want to sleep on paper towels on the bottom of his cage because his feet may pain him somewhat. If the older bird lives with other younger birds, keep an eye on him so that they don't pick on him if he becomes infirm or ill. Watch his general condition so that you can catch any health problems early.

Feeling Good

Chapter 6

Being Good

There's no such thing as a "bad" parakeet, just an untamed one that isn't socialized to humans. Untamed birds may bite and try to flee when you attempt to handle them simply because they aren't used to that kind of attention. They aren't misbehaved—they just haven't learned yet that you aren't going to harm them.

When most people discuss training their parakeet, what they really mean is taming. Training involves an end result behavior and a process based on learning theories. Taming is simply socialization. You will discover how to do both in this chapter.

Parakeets can be trained to perform simple behaviors; however, it's more likely that your bird will train you than the other way around. Parakeets learn quickly what works to get what they want. If your bird is begging to be let out of his cage with high-pitched whistles and a frantic dance in front of his door, and then you open the cage, he will learn that the behavior works. This is called "positive reinforcement," and it is the basis for effective taming or training.

Positive Reinforcement

Positive reinforcement behavior modification is based on the theory that animals (including humans) will continue to perform a behavior that works to achieve a certain goal. When a behavior doesn't prove to be effective, the animal will usually try something different to see if the new behavior works. When you reward desired behaviors and ignore unwanted ones, you are reinforcing the desired behavior and making it more likely that it will happen again.

For example, let's say that the bird wants to get out of the cage to play, so he bounces around the door making noise. You let him out because the "dance" is so cute. He will do that dance again to try to get you to let him out again. If it works, the behavior will continue to be reinforced until it doesn't work anymore. If you stop letting him out when he does the dance, the

Before you begin taming or training your parakeet, you must first establish a relationship with him.

behavior will eventually become extinct and he will try something else. This is the basis for the kind of taming and training that works best with parakeets.

For taming and training to work, you must first develop a relationship with your parakeet. Don't force him to do anything he doesn't want to do, and respect him as you would a good friend. A bird that sees his guardian as a friend is more likely to become tame. Fear tactics don't work with birds, but gentle, patient training methods do. Speak softly to him and handle him tenderly. Know your parakeet's limitations before you set out to teach him complicated behaviors, and don't push anything on him before he's ready.

Socialization

Socialization is the process by which you introduce your bird to everything he will encounter in the household or outside. If you do this while he's young, he will grow up unafraid of the objects of everyday life. An older bird that has not been socialized to household items will fear them, and he may not ever get used to things like the vacuum cleaner, household pets, or strangers. However, parakeets are much less wary of these things than some larger species and are pretty easygoing about items that are new to the environment.

To socialize the bird to odd objects, like the vacuum cleaner, begin by placing the object across the room. Or, if the item is eventually to be inside the parakeet's cage, like a new perch that he might be scared of, place it on a table just a few feet from the cage where he can easily see it. Every two to three days, move the object a little closer to the cage. Don't rush. Allow the bird to begin to accept the item in his environment. In the case of the vacuum cleaner or other noise-making objects, you will have to move the item closer until it's right next to the cage

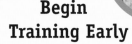

The Expert Knows

Begin Training Early

Before you begin taming or training your parakeet, he must be comfortable in his new surroundings, as well as comfortable with you. The key to training a bird—or any animal—is trust. Once he has adjusted, you can begin to hand-tame him. Beginning early is also essential. Whether you have a young bird or an older one, start training him a week to ten days after bringing him home because the longer you wait, the more difficult it will be. An untamed adult is not a hopeless case; the process will just take longer and require more patience.

Being Good

for a few days, but then start back at stage one when you're going to begin turning it on. Most parakeets don't have issues with many household objects, so you won't have to do much of this.

Other pets, especially dogs, cats, and other predators, can be scary for a new bird. Eventually, the bird will get used to the presence of these other animals. Make sure that his cage is very secure and that the other pets can't get into it or knock it over. Don't try to do face-to-face introductions with dogs and cats. To them, the parakeet probably looks like a fun toy or treat. Parakeets are in grave danger with cats around, so take extreme precaution that that cats can't get anywhere near the birdcage.

Introducing the bird to the human members of the family is easier. Don't pull the bird out on the first day home and pass him around—he's not a puppy! He has to get used to his new housing, environment, other pets, and new people. If he's alone, he probably isn't used to being without other birds. Play the radio or TV for him so that he has some noise in his environment— he's used to that from the pet store or breeder. Parakeets don't like dead silence during the day.

After a couple of days, have everyone begin approaching the cage and speaking softly or singing to the bird. After a few more days, people can begin offering millet spray through the bars and encouraging the bird to take a few nibbles. The idea is to do this very slowly so that the bird engages with everyone in a positive manner; if someone scares him, his taming will be set back.

One way to earn the trust of your parakeet is to offer tasty food rewards for good behaviors.

Taming

A very young parakeet is easy to handle because he's far less likely to bite and is more apt to be gentle and willing to try new things. Handle your youngster every day starting with the day after you bring him home. Have him stand in the palm of your hand or on your finger. Don't press him to do more than he's prepared to do. For example, this isn't the time to train him to stay on a play gym. Instead, sit on the floor in a safe room and have him perch on your shoulder, a very secure area, or on your finger with your hand close to your chest. Talk and whistle to him. Put him back after about ten minutes, and repeat several times a day. Make these handling sessions relaxing and fun for him. If he becomes stressed when you're handling him, he won't want to come out of the cage for you, and he'll begin to use his only two modes of defense—fight (biting) and flight (flapping around the cage).

A semi-tame parakeet may have been handled before, but also may be mistrustful of humans. The main problem with the semi-tame bird is that he's not tame enough to have meaningful interactions with you yet, but he's tame enough to get near your hand to bite it. But, you can tame this bird easily if you take some simple steps toward developing a trusting relationship with him.

There are two basic ways to tame a parakeet, similar to how you'd train a

Carrier Training

Most parakeets will acclimate easily to a travel carrier and don't need a lot of socialization with it. Simply put it near the cage and include it in playtime, putting the bird inside and then taking him right out again. Put some toys in and on top of the carrier, and allow him to play there. When you travel, include some millet spray, seed, and a very shallow dish of water. A water bottle is recommended, but if your parakeet isn't used to drinking from one, he may not know how and will dehydrate. Put paper towels on the bottom of the carrier so that the bird has good footing. Don't include a perch, but you can include a rolled up washcloth for the bird to stand on.

horse—you can "break" him or you can "gentle" him. Using a gentle, slow training method is always preferable with an animal as sensitive as this one. "Breaking" a parakeet using quick, forceful training, will work for a time, but does not allow a real bond to form.

Give your semi-tame parakeet a period of adjustment when you first

> *Hand-taming and training will be most successful if you are patient and gentle at all times.*

94

Parakeets

bring him home. He will be stressed in his new situation. Do not consider taming him until he has settled into a routine. This may take a few days to

Flown the Coop?

Open windows and doors and an unclipped parakeet are a match for disaster. Prevent the loss of your bird by adding screens to your windows and making sure he's caged before opening any doors. Never take him outside unless you're positive that he has a very good clip, or he's in a safe carrier. If you do lose your bird, hunt for him outside, clicking and calling his name. Tell all of your neighbors and make up posters offering a reward. Call all of the vets and animal shelters in the area. Finally, cross your fingers.

more than a week. Once a parakeet is eating well, vocalizing, preening, and bathing, he is adjusted to his new home, and you can begin with short taming sessions.

Once your new bird is settled in, you will first need to clip his wings if they aren't clipped already. A parakeet with free flight will fly away from you and not return for the taming session! Even if you want to allow your bird to fly eventually, you will have to clip his wings during the training period; the feathers will grow back in time.

Untamed or semi-tame, fish your bird out of his cage with a small washcloth and hold him gently to prevent him from biting you. He may scream and struggle, but be calm and talk to him in a soothing voice. Take him to a small, safe room—the bathroom is ideal—but close the toilet lid and remove any dangerous items that may fall and break if he comes in contact with them. Ideally, the room should be somewhat dimly lit, but not dark.

Sit on the floor with your knees bent into "mountains" in front of you, and place the bird gently on top of your knees, holding him there for a moment before you let go. The minute you let go, the bird will probably flutter away from you. Gather up the bird and try to place him on your knee again. Repeat this action until he eventually stands for a moment on your knee. He may not want to stay there in the first few sessions, but keep trying. Do this two or three times a day for 10 to 20 minutes each session, but no more than that.

Once you've gotten your bird to stand on your knee, talk to him in a very calm voice and begin to move one hand slowly up your leg toward him. Little by little, session after session, move your hand slowly up your leg until the bird allows it to come very close. The idea

here is that he should eventually allow contact with your hand. This may take quite a while, so be patient. Once the bird allows your hand to approach closely, try to tickle his chest with your finger or scratch his head and neck if he allows, still moving very slowly. If he is particularly skittish, move a millet spray up your leg toward him before you offer your hand. It's a great sign if he nibbles on the spray. After a few sessions, you can begin to try to get the bird to stand on your hand.

At the end of the training session, place your parakeet back in his cage. If you have trouble with that, put your hand gently over the bird's back so he can't open his wings to try to fly away or attempt to climb on the outside of the cage.

An untamed parakeet is one that has not had much, if any, handling by humans. He is fearful of humans and can be aggressive, but he's not impossible to tame. After letting him adjust to his new home, you have to show him that you aren't afraid of him. If you are bitten and you retreat, you show him that he has an

Although training is a gradual process, most parakeets catch on quickly and will soon allow you to handle them.

Rewards Get Results

You might need to give your parakeet a little more motivation during taming or training sessions, so try to find a food that he will do anything to get. Most are very attracted to millet spray. As you get to know your bird, you'll discover what he likes. The ideal treat is anything he will rush to get. You will give him just a taste, then pull the treat away until the next time he does something right. Reward desired behaviors as much as possible for the best results. Don't be stingy with praise or treats!

effective tool for making you go away. The best way to deal with biting is to avoid being bitten. This means that you may want to work with stick training before you begin using your hands (you'll get directions for stick training later in the chapter). Don't use gloves—you want the bird to become used to hands, and using gloves defeats that.

Be Patient!

You can't tame a frightened or ill bird. Your parakeet will be best tamed when he is content and relaxed. Signs of a happy and calm bird are: preening and grooming, fluffing feathers, yawning, being playful, and showing a lot of interest in what you're doing. Most importantly, never yell at or punish your parakeet—it won't work and will damage any trust that you have established. Be patient, keep training sessions short, and have unrealistic expectations.

If your parakeet is extremely untamed, you can hold him properly and gently in a towel and talk softly to him while caressing his head. Do this twice a day for the first few days before you begin training him. Your parakeet does not like to be restrained like this, but he will come to understand that you aren't hurting him, even though being restrained is uncomfortable. Use this method *only* if you are certain that holding your parakeet is not causing him pain or undue stress, and do it only for a few minutes at a time.

Step-Up and Stick Training

Of all the behaviors you can teach your parakeet, "step-up" is the most important. This behavior allows you to retrieve your parakeet at any time and is especially useful when he's in danger. Step-up is when your parakeet steps gently on to your hand or finger without hesitating. It's important to reinforce this command so that it becomes second nature to your bird. If he's used to standing on your finger or a stick, he's more likely to do it when you require. Fortunately, this behavior comes very naturally to parrots, so teaching it to a tame bird is a breeze.

Assuming that you're teaching a tame or semi-tame parakeet the step-up behavior, begin by allowing him to come out of his cage on his own. If he will step onto your hand, bring him out that way—you're on the right track to reinforcing this behavior. Place a perch on top of his cage, or place him onto a play gym where he will be standing on a round dowel, not a flat surface.

Give him a treat like millet spray. Next, begin rubbing your bird's chest and belly very softly and gently with the length of your index finger, talking to him soothingly, slowly increasing the

pressure with which you push on his chest. If he steps onto your hand, praise him and then put him back on the perch and repeat. If he doesn't step up, you can increase the pressure. Pushing slightly on a parakeet's chest throws him off balance, so he will lift up a foot to right himself. Place your finger or hand under the foot and lift him, if he allows it. If not, simply allow his foot to remain on your hand until he removes it. As you do this, tell your bird clearly to "step-up." Always say "step-up" when he steps on to your hand so that he comes to associate the behavior with the words.

Once your parakeet is fairly good at stepping up, have him step from finger to finger, repeating the phrase "step-up," and praising him when he performs. He may hesitate at first, but soon he'll know exactly what you want. Perching is a natural behavior. Be sure that your training sessions last only a few minutes each, and incorporate them into playtime. Try not to become frustrated if your parakeet doesn't do exactly what you want right away. Most youngsters will learn the step-up behavior easily, in one or two short sessions, though a semi-tame parakeet may take longer. The more your bird trusts you, the easier it is to teach him anything. Even if the step-up behavior is the

Of all the behaviors you can teach your parakeet, "step-up" is the most important.

only "trick" you teach him, is it by far the most valuable.

Stick training is simply teaching the "step-up" behavior using a perch or dowel instead of your finger. It's critical that your parakeet know how to step onto a stick. The day may come when he refuses to come down from the curtain rod, or gets out of the house and is sitting in the branches of a tree. A parakeet that has been stick trained will be easier to retrieve with a long dowel or broomstick. One that isn't used to stepping onto a stick will be terrified of it, and, as a result, you may lose the opportunity to save your bird.

Teach "step-up" with a stick the same way you teach it with your finger. Stick training should begin as soon as you begin hand-taming your parakeet. If your bird is terrified of the stick, leave it close to the cage where he will have a chance to view it and get used to its presence. Move it closer and closer, and eventually put it on top of the cage, and then into the cage before training with it. Allow the bird to live with it for awhile. Use different types of sticks during training, so that your parakeet is

If your parakeet becomes tired or frustrated during training, you should put him back in his cage for a rest.

comfortable with various dowels and perches.

"Whittle-Down" Training Method

Being afraid of your parakeet's beak is understandable, but they don't pack much of a bite. If you want to avoid being bitten, try the "whittle-down" taming method. Begin by stick training your bird with the step-up command using a 12 to 18 inch (30.5 to 45.7 cm) dowel or perch that's an appropriately sized width for a parakeet. Once your bird learns to step on to the stick and does it with ease, begin cutting the stick shorter, about an inch each week, until the stick is very short. Eventually, if you've done this slowly enough and have worked to gain your bird's trust, the

stick will be so short that he will naturally step onto your hand.

Talking

Parakeets are arguably the best talkers in the parrot family, able to learn hundreds of words and phrases, perhaps even thousands. They don't speak as clearly as other, larger parrots, but their vocabulary can be massive. Teaching your parakeet to talk is pretty easy, but it can take some time. Some gifted parakeets will learn to talk in just a few weeks, and others may not talk for a year. Repetition, repetition, repetition—that's just about all you need to know.

Your parakeet's first attempts at talking will sound garbled. Once this "baby talk" begins, you'll start to hear words becoming clearer. This is the time to correct your bird's pronunciation, repeating the phrases that he's attempting (if you understand them) the way they should sound. You'll be surprised at how clearly your parakeet will begin to repeat words if you teach him how they're meant to be pronounced.

Pairs are less likely to talk than the single bird, and single birds with mirrors are often less likely to talk than single birds without mirrors. If a parakeet has something to talk to, he won't likely talk to you. But, it's sad to force a bird to be lonely so that he'll talk, so you may need a compromise. Wait until your bird learns to talk, and

Don't Do List

There are a few things you should never do during training. Do not "punish" or discipline a parakeet—it will only ruin the bond of trust between you if you do. Here's a list of parakeet "nevers":

- Never hit, flick, squeeze, or throw your parakeet. This is animal abuse.
- Never hold or flick the beak. It is very sensitive!
- Never throw anything at your parakeet's cage to make him stop vocalizing. This will make him feel very insecure.
- Never "play rough."
- Never cover the cage for long periods during the day. If you have a sleeping infant or you need your bird to quiet down, cover it for an hour or so. It's cruel to cover the cage for extended periods when your parakeet should be active.
- Never starve your parakeet as a training tool. He has a fast metabolism and can die if prevented from eating for a day or two.

then get him a friend or mirror toy to pal around with.

Learning to talk is a parakeet's way of attempting to communicate with the rest of the household. Talking indicates a deep affection for his guardians, or at least a heightened attentiveness. The more attention and affection you lavish on your bird, the more likely he is to talk to you.

Male parakeets speak with more frequency and will learn more words than females. There are exceptions, of course, but this is the general rule. Females do become capable whistlers, however, so don't worry—they will mimic sounds they hear. If you really want your parakeet to talk, don't teach him to whistle first. Whistling is easier and more fun, apparently, than talking. You can teach your bird to whistle after he has learned several phrases. Of course, if you have a female, you can teach whistling from the beginning.

The only way to teach your bird to talk is to repeat yourself a lot. A parakeet has to hear a word or phrase many times before he masters it. Most birds learn things their guardians say to them every

Birdie Words

Talking is a parakeet's way of trying to communicate with you and learning your language. It indicates a deep affection, or at least a heightened attentiveness, toward you, the owner. The more attention and affection you lavish on your parakeet, the more likely he will be to talk to you. Also, saying words or phrases with energy and enthusiasm is interesting to your parakeet. This is why greetings, names, commands, and those words you shouldn't say seem easier for him learn. Teaching your parakeet to talk can be an enjoyable activity for both you and your bird.

FAMILY-FRIENDLY TIP

Kids and Training

Children, in particular, must be trained to handle a parakeet gently and with composure. Always supervise young children while they are handling birds, especially during training. Though a parakeet's bite may not hurt an adult much, it can definitely break the skin of a child's hand. Make sure the bird is tame before training sessions begin. Youngsters can offer treats and sing to calm the bird. Teach them not to move quickly or make fast hand motions while doing so.

learning intricate behaviors. The best way to teach tricks is to capitalize on natural behaviors and rewarding the ones you like. For example, if you notice that your parakeet is great at climbing, place him on the end of a long piece of rope and encourage him to climb up, praising him in a high-pitched voice when he completes the task—placing a millet spray at the top of the rope doesn't hurt. If he jumps off before he reaches the top, then start again, this time encouraging him and praising when he's climbing, and stopping when he jumps off. Remember, whenever you want to teach your parakeet anything, use a lot of praise and make the training session fun. Also, if you can find a treat that your parakeet

day, such as their name, good morning, good night, pretty bird, want some food, and so on. Once you've decided on a phrase you want your parakeet to learn, say it over and over every time you pass the cage, and be sure to say it clearly so that he will hear it correctly. Words with hard sounds like p, t, c, k, b, and d are easiest to learn.

Tricks

Parakeets can be taught simple tricks, but they are not known to be proficient at

The best way to teach your parakeet simple tricks is to reinforce natural behaviors, like climbing and nodding.

Being Good

adores, millet spray, for example, use it in your training sessions rather than just offering it freely in the cage.

Problem Behaviors

Though there aren't "problem parakeets," there are problem behaviors that you can resolve either through behavior modification, boosting the bird's health, or changing the way the bird lives in order to make the behavior cease. Here are a few behaviors that guardians often complain about.

Biting

Biting occurs when a bird is fearful and feeling cornered. He doesn't want the type of attention you're offering. Parakeets also bite when they're protecting their cage, mate, or nest. Consider what's going on at the time. Are you trying to handle an untamed bird? Are you trying to pick up a bird that's protecting eggs? Begin with the basics of socialization and taming to resolve the problem.

If a previously tame bird starts biting, he or she may have a health issue or is becoming hormonal, or perhaps the bird has been left alone so long that he has reverted in his training. Maybe something has traumatized him and he no longer wants a human hand near him. Try to see it from his point of view.

If you determine that he's healthy, you can potentially get him to stop biting by moving his cage, or moving around the toys and perches inside the cage. Sometimes a little change of scenery helps. For playtime, remove the bird from the room where his cage is, and try handling him in a safe place which he's not all that familiar with.

Screaming

Parakeets chitter-chatter and sing for most of the day, and there's not much you're going to be able to do about it. They are not notorious screamers and generally don't annoy the household or the neighbors. If you hear genuine screaming from your parakeet, he

Many problem behaviors can be resolved by simply changing the way your bird lives or by boosting his health.

might have his toe or head caught in a toy, or perhaps he has injured himself or something is scaring him.

Chewing

Parakeets love to chew, especially on soft wood and paper. Chewing generally isn't a problem as long as you give your bird safe toys to chew on. If you allow your parakeet out inside your home, watch him carefully to make sure he doesn't get into anything he can bite on, such as houseplants, picture frames, and so on. You're not going to prevent him from chewing; you can only prevent him from getting to the items he wants to chew.

Feather Plucking

A parakeet that's plucking his feathers out or is chewing them and becomes scruffy and fluffy looking has a serious problem. Like other parrots, parakeets can begin feather mutilation due to boredom, but this behavior is more likely due to illness or a skin condition. See a veterinarian immediately if you notice bald patches or fluffy patches; a healthy molting bird will lose feathers gradually all over his body, not in patches.

Most problem behaviors are easily resolved. The better you know your bird, the more you will be able to do to keep him healthy and happy. Along with proper care, daily training sessions will strengthen the bond between you and your parakeet.

Body Language

Parakeets have a unique body language. Here are a few things to look out for:

- **Sleeping posture:** A healthy parakeet will sleep on one foot, with the other tucked into his belly; his head will either be tucked into his neck, or turned around and resting on his back.
- **Wing flapping:** Also called wing drumming, this is when a bird stands on his perch and flaps his wings wildly, a sign he is content or communicating with you.
- **Regurgitating:** A high compliment, this happens when birds feed one another or their chicks regurgitated food; birds that are very affectionate with their humans may also do this with a person, or with a favored toy.
- **Beak grinding:** You may hear your bird make a little grinding noise with his beak before he falls asleep; this is a sign of comfort and contentment.

Resources

Clubs and Societies

American Federation of Aviculture, Inc.
P.O. Box 7312
N. Kansas City, MO 64116
Phone:(816) 421-2473
Fax: (816) 421-3214
afaoffice@aol.com
www.AFAbirds.org

Avicultural Society of America
Secretary: Helen Hanson
info@asabirds.org
www.asabirds.org

Budgerigar Association of America
Secretary: Kerry Laverty
pro@applink.net
www.budgerigarassociation.com

The American Budgerigar Society
Secretary: Diane Ingram
abssecretary@cs.com
www.abs1.org

Veterinary Resources

Academy of Veterinary Homeopathy (AVH)
P.O. Box 9280
Wilmington, DE 19809
www.theavh.org

American Academy of Veterinary Acupuncture (AAVA)
66 Morris Avenue, Suite 2A
Springfield, NJ 07081
E-mail: office@aava.org
www.aava.org

American Animal Hospital Association (AAHA)
P.O. Box 150899
Denver, CO 80215-0899
E-mail: info@aahanet.org
www.aahanet.org/Index.cfm

American College of Veterinary Internal Medicine (ACVIM)
1997 Wadsworth Blvd., Suite A
Lakewood, CO 80214-5293
Phone: (800) 245-9081
Fax: (303) 231-0880
Email: ACVIM@ACVIM.org
www.acvim.org

American College of Veterinary Ophthalmologists (ACVO)
P.O. Box 1311
Meridian, Idaho 83860
Phone: (208) 466-7624
Fax: (208) 466-7693
E-mail: office@acvo.com
www.acvo.com

American Holistic Veterinary Medical Association (AHVMA)
2218 Old Emmorton Road
Bel Air, MD 21015
E-mail: office@ahvma.org
www.ahvma.org

American Veterinary Chiropractic Association (AVCA)
442154 E 140 Rd.
Bluejacket, OK 74333
Phone: (918) 784-2231
E-mail: amvetchiro@aol.com
www.animalchiropractic.org

American Veterinary Medical Association (AVMA)
1931 North Meacham Road-Suite 100
Schaumburg, IL 60173
E-mail: avmainfo@avma.org
www.avma.org

Animal Behavior Society
Indiana University
2611 East 10th Street #170
Bloomington IN 47408-2603
Phone: (812) 856-5541
E-mail: aboffice@indiana.edu
www.animalbehavior.org

Association of Avian Veterinarians (AAV)
P.O. Box 811720
Boca Raton, FL 33481-1720
Phone: (561) 393-8901
Fax: (561) 393-8902
AAVCTRLOFC@aol.com
www.aav.org

British Veterinary Association (BVA)
7 Mansfield Street
London
W1G 9NQ
Telephone: 020 7636 6541
Fax: 020 7436 2970
E-mail: bvahq@bva.co.uk
www.bva.co.uk

International Veterinary Acupuncture Society (IVAS)
P.O. Box 271395
Ft. Collins, CO 80527-1395
E-mail: office@ivas.org
www.ivas.org/main.cfm

Orthopedic Foundation for Animals (OFA)
2300 NE Nifong Blvd
Columbus, Missouri 65201-3856
Phone: (573) 442-0418
Fax: (573) 875-5073
Email: ofa@offa.org
www.offa.org

Emergency Resources

ASPCA Animal Poison Control Center
Phone:(888) 426-4435
napcc@aspca.org (for general information only)
www.apcc.aspca.org

Bird Hotline
P.O. Box 1411
Sedona, AZ 86339-1411
birdhotline@birdhotline.com
www.birdhotline.com

Rescue and Adoption Organizations

American Humane Association (AHA)
63 Inverness Drive East
Englewood, CO 80112
Phone: (303) 792-9900
Fax: 792-5333
www.americanhumane.org

American Society for the Prevention of Cruelty to Animals (ASPCA)
424 E. 92nd Street
New York, NY 10128-6804
Phone: (212) 876-7700
www.aspca.org

Best Friends Animal Sanctuary
5001 Angel Canyon Road
Kanab, UT 84741-5001
Phone: (435) 644-2001
info@bestfriends.org
www.bestfriends.com/

Bird Placement Program
P.O. Box 347392
Parma, OH, 44134-7392
Phone: (330) 772-1627
www.avi-sci.com/bpp/

Caged Bird Rescue
911 Thomson Road
Pegram, TN 37143
Phone: (615) 646-3949

Exotic Bird Rescue Ring
www.neebs.org/birdresc.htm

Feathered Friends Adoption and Rescue Program
East Coast Headquarters
4751 Ecstasy Circle
Cocoa, FL, 32926
Phone: (407) 633-4744
West Coast Branch
Phone: (941) 764-6048
members.aol.com/_ht_a/MAHorton/FFAP.html

For the Love of Parrots Refuge Society
3450 Interporvincial Highway
Abbotsford, British Columbia
Phone: (604) 854-8180
or (604) 854-8381

Foster Parrots Ltd.
P.O. Box 650
Rockland, MA, 02370
Phone: (781) 878-3733
www.fosterparrots.com

Gabriel Foundation
P.O. Box 11477
Aspen, CO 81612
Phone: (877) 923-1009
www.thegabrielfoundation.org

Oasis Sanctuary
P.O. Box 3104
Scottsdale, AZ 85271
www.the-oasis.org/

Northcoast Bird Adoption and Rehabilitation Center, Inc. (NBARC)
P.O. Box 367
Aurora, OH
Phone: (330) 425-9269
or (330) 562-6999
www.adoptabird.com

Parrot Education and Adoption Center (PEAC)
P.O. Box 34501
San Diego, CA
Phone: 92163-4501, (619) 232-2409
www.peac.org

Royal Society for the Prevention of Cruelty to Animals (RSPCA)
Phone: 0870 3335 999
Fax: 0870 7530 284
www.rspca.org.uk

Tucson Avian Rescue and Adoption (TARA)
Phone: (520) 531-9305
or (520) 322-9685
www.found-pets.org/tara.html

The Blue Cross
Shilton Road
Burford
Oxon OX18 4PF
England
Phone: 44 01993 825500
info@bluecross.org.uk
www.bluecross.org.uk/

The Fund for Animals
200 West 57th Street
New York, NY 10019
Phone: (212) 246-2096
fundinfo@fund.org
www.fund.org

The Humane Society of the United States (HSUS)
2100 L Street, NW
Washington DC 20037
Phone: (202) 452-1100
www.hsus.org

Tropics Exotic Bird Refuge
P.O. Box 686
Kannapolis, NC 28082-0686
Phone: (704) 932-8041
or (704) 634-9066
tropics@juno.com

Websites

Avian Rescue Online
www.avianrescue.org

Birdy Works
www.birdyworks.com

Budgerigars Galore
www.budgerigars.co.uk

Budgerigar Home Page
www.geocities.com/RainForest/3298

Budgerigar Society
www.budgerigarsociety.com

Budgerigar World
www.tuxford.dabsol.co.uk

Healthypet
www.healthypet.com

Master Budgerigar Breeder
www.tuxford.dabsol.co.uk/masterbreeder/
home.htm

Pets 911
www.1888pets911.org

World of Budgerigars
www.budgerigarworld.com/piriquito/Breeders
/BreedersHomePages.htm

World Parrot Trust
www.worldparrottrust.org

VetQuest
www.vin.com/vetquest/index0.html

Publications

Magazines
Bird Talk
3 Burroughs
Irvine, CA 92618
Phone: (949) 855-8822
www.animalnetwork.com/birdtalk/default.asp

Bird Times
7-L Dundas Circle
Greensboro, NC 27407
Phone: (336)292-4047
Budgerigar World
budgerigarworld@msn.com
www.budgerigarworld.com

Good Bird
PO Box 684394
Austin, TX 78768
Phone: (512) 423-7734
or (512) 236-0531
info@goodbirdinc.com
www.GoodBirdInc.com

Pet Bird Report
2236 Mariner Square Drive, No. 35
Alameda, CA 94501
Phone: (510) 523-5303
www.petbirdreport.com

Winged Wisdom
Birds n Ways
39760 Calle Bellagio
Temecula, CA 92592
Phone: (909) 303-9376

Books
Moustaki, Nikki, *Parakeets*,
TFH Publications.
Moustaki, Nikki, *Your Outta Control
Bird*, TFH Publications.

Parakeets

Index

A

acidophilus, 57
adoption organizations, 106–107
African lovebirds, 7
aspergillosis infection, 82–83
Australia and the parakeet, 6
availability of food, 45

B

baby birds
    feeding, 14
    hand-feeding, 14
    socialization in, 91–92
    taming, 93–96, 94, 95
bacterial infections, 84
barring, head, 17
bathing and bathing dishes, 38,
    61–62
beak care, 64–65, 75–76
bedding, 36
Belgium and the parakeet, 8
bird seed, 43–46, 44
bird-proofing your home, 27
biting, 102
bleeding from broken feathers,
    77–78
body language of parakeet, 103
bones, 79
breathing, 78
breeding, 8, 15–16
    color variations and, 8–9
    egg binding in, 85–86
    leg banding and, 16–17, 17
    lighting requirements
        and, 16
    preventing unwanted, 86
    reproductive disorders
        and, 85–86
    testicular tumors and, 86
broken feathers, 77–78
budgies, 6
bumblefoot, 86

C

cages. *See* housing
calcium in diet, 34, 42
canned fruits and vegetables, 51–52
caring for your parakeet, 18
carrier training, 93
cere, 11, 19
changing foods, 47
chewing, 103
children and parakeets, 13, 38,
    55, 63, 68, 73, 90, 101

cleaning and maintenance of cages,
    37
clipping wings, 65–69, 66–67
clubs and societies for
    parakeet fanciers, 9–10, 104
coloration, 8–9, 10–11
cooked diets, 52
covers for cages, 35, 38
cups and bowls, 28–30, 29
cuttlebones and mineral
    blocks, 34–35

D

dietary supplements and,
    56–57
digestive system, 79–80
don't do list, in training your ....
    parakeet, 99

E

ears, 11–12, 75
egg binding, 85–86
eggs (cooked) in diet, 53–54
emergency resources, 105–106
England and the parakeet, 8
English budgie vs. parakeet,
    9–10, 11
exercise for health, 85
eyes, 11, 17, 19, 75

F

feathers, 12, 60, 76–78
    bleeding from broken,
        77–78
    chewing or plucking of,
        77, 103
    molting or loss of, 61, 69,
        76, 77
    oil residue on, cleaning, 77
    wing clipping and, 65–69,
        66–67
feeding, 41–57
    availability of food in, 45
    bird seed in, 43–46, 44
    calcium in, 34, 42
    changing foods and, 47
    cooked diets in, 52
    cups and bowls in, 28–30, 29
    dietary supplements and,
        56–57
    digestive system and, 79, 81
    eggs (cooked) in, 53–54
    grit for digestion and, 46
    hand-, for babies, 14

kabobs in, 52
natural diet of parakeet
    and, 7, 43
pelleted foods in, 46–48, 46
pesticides in, 48
sample diets in, 54–56
table foods in, 53–54
toxic foods products and, 51
treats in, 54
variety in, 43
vegetables and fruit in,
    48–52, 50t
vitamins A and C in, 42
water requirements and, 54
feet, 12, 76
first-aid kit, 80
flying your parakeet, 23
France and the parakeet, 8
free-range vs. caging your
    parakeet, 22–23, 27
    playtime for, 34
    wing clipping and, 65–69,
        66–67
fruit in diet, 48–52, 50t
fungal infections, 82–83
furnishings and accessories for
cage, 28, 28

G

Germany and the parakeet, 8
giardia infection, 82
gout, 86
grapefruit seed extract, 57
grit for digestion, 46
grooming, 59–69
    bathing and bathing
        dishes for, 38, 61–62
    beak care in, 64–65
    feather loss or molts and,
        61, 69, 76, 77
    feathers and, 60
    health check during, 65,
        74
    nail care and, 63–64, 63
    oil gland and, 60
    supplies for, 64
    wing clipping and, 65–69,
        66–67

H

habitats for parakeet, 26
hand-feeding babies, 14
head barring, 17
health issues, 71–87

administering medication in, 84
aspergillosis infection and, 82-83
bacterial infections in, 84
beak and, 75-76
bleeding from broken feathers and, 77-78
bones and, 79
broken feathers, 77-78
bumblefoot in, 86
calcium in, 42
chewing or plucking feathers in, 77, 103
cuttlebones and mineral blocks in, 34-35
dietary supplements and, 56-57
digestive system and, 79, 81
ears and, 75
egg binding in, 85-86
exercise and, 85
eyes and, 75
feathers and, 76-78
feet and, 76
first-aid kit for, 80
fungal infections in, 82
giardia infection and, 82
gout in, 86
grit for digestion and, 46
grooming and, as health check, 65, 74
harmful or toxic items and, 39, 78, 86
heat stress and, 78-79
hospital cage for, 76
lameness in, 86
life span and, 16, 18
megabacteria infection in, 84
mites and, 81-82
molting and, 61, 69, 76, 77
musculoskeletal system and, 79
Pacheco's disease in, 84-85
polyoma virus infection in, 84
psittacine beak and feather disease (PBFD) in, 84
psittacosis (parrot fever) in, 83-84
quarantine of sick birds and, 83
reproductive disorders and, 85-86
respiratory system and, 78
senior birds and, 87
signs and symptoms recognition in, 73-74, 85

stress and, 81
toy safety and, 31
tuberculosis in, 83
tumors and, 86
veterinarian selection and vet visits in, 72-73, 104-105
viral diseases in, 84-85
vitamins A and C in, 42
wing clipping and, 65-69, 66-67
worms and worming in, 82
yeast infections in, 83
heat stress, 78-79
history of the parakeet, 6-7
Holland and the parakeet, 8
homemade toys, 32
hospital cage, 76
housing and cages, 22-39
    alternatives to cages as, 26
    bathing dishes for, 38
    bedding in, 36
    bird-proofing your home and, 27
    cleaning and maintenance of, 37
    covers for, 35, 38
    cups and bowls in, 28-30, 29
    cuttlebones and mineral blocks in, 34-35
    free-range vs., 22-23, 27
    furnishings and accessories ... for, 28, 28
    habitats for, 26
    harmful or toxic items and, ... 39, 78
    hospital cages and, 76
    lighting requirements and, 35-36
    materials used in, 23-25
    perches in, 32-34, 33
    placement/location of, 25-26
    play gyms and, 34, 35
    safety vs. design of, 25
    seed catchers for, 36
    size of, 23
    toys and, 29, 30-32, 30
    travel carriers and, 39

I
import of birds to U.S. and Europe, 6, 8
intelligence, 11, 14-15
Internet resources, 107-108
J
Japan and the parakeet, 9

K
kabobs, 52

L
lameness, 86
leg banding, 16-17, 17
life span, 16, 18
lighting requirements, 35-36
    breeding and, 16
    cage covers and, 35, 38
lost birds, 94

M
materials used in cages, 23-25
megabacteria infection, 84
Melopsittacus undulatus, 7
mineral blocks, 34-35
mite protectors, 39
mites, 81-82
molting, 61, 69, 76, 77
multiple parakeet, 16
musculoskeletal system, 79

N
nail care, 63-64, 63
names of the parakeet, 7
nares, 11
National Animal Poison Control Hotlines, 86
natural habitat of parakeet, 6
nonstick cookware and toxic fumes, 78

O
oil gland, 60

P
Pacheco's disease, 84-85
parrot fever (psittacosis), 83-84
parrots vs. parakeet, 6
pastimes for parakeet, 29
pelleted foods, 46-48, 46
perches, 15, 32-34, 33
    warming type, 33-34
pesticides, 48
physical characteristics, 10-12
placement/location of cages, 25-26
play gyms and, 34, 35
Poison Control Hotline, 86
poisonous materials, 39, 51, 78, 86
polyoma virus infection, 84
positive reinforcement training, 90-91
probiotics, 57
problem behaviors, 102
    biting, 102
    chewing, 103
    feather plucking, 103
    screaming, 102-103, 102
Psittacidae family, 6

psittacine beak and feather disease (PBFD), 84
psittacosis (parrot fever), 83–84
publications, books, magazines, 108

Q

quarantine of sick birds, 83

R

reproductive disorders, 85–86
rescue and adoption organizations, 106–107
resources, 104–108
respiratory system, 78
roundworms, 82

S

safety of toys, 31
safety vs. design of cages, 25
sample diets, 54–56
screaming, 102–103
seed catchers, 36
senior birds, health care for, 87
showering with your parakeet, 39
size of cage, 23
socialization, 91–92
spangle coloration, 9
spirulina, 57
step-up training, 96–98
stick training, 96–98
stress and illness, 81
supplements, 56–57
symptoms recognition in illness, 73–74, 85

T

table foods in diet, 53–54
talking, training your parakeet to, 14, 99–101
taming your parakeet, 93–96, 94, 95
temperament and behavior, 6, 13–14
testicular tumors, 86
toxic items, 39, 51, 78, 86
toys, 29, 30–32, 30
training, 89–102
    body language of parakeet and, 103
    carrier training and, 93
    don't do list, 99
    positive reinforcement in, 90–91
    problem behaviors and. *See* ... problem behaviors
    socialization in, 91–92
    step-up command in, 96–98
    stick training in, 96–98
    talking, 14, 99–101
    taming to hand, 93–96, 94, 95
    treats in, 92, 96
    tricks, 101–102
    whistling, 100
    "whittle-down" method in, 98
travel carriers, 39
treats, 54, 92, 96
tricks to teach your parakeet, 101–102
tube-style waterers for, 28–30, 29
tuberculosis, 83

tumors, 86

U

United States and the parakeet, 6, 9

V

vegetables and fruit in diet, 48–52, 50t
vent, 13
veterinarian selection and vet visits, 72–73, 104–105
viral diseases, 84–85
vitamins A and C, 42
vocalizations and calls, 13–14

W

water requirements, 6, 7, 54
    cups, bowls, and tube-style waterers for, 28–30, 29
websites of interest, 107–108
whistling training, 100
"whittle-down" training method, 98
wild parakeets, 9
wing clipping and, 65–69, 66–67
worms and worming, 82

Y

yeast infections, 83

111

Index

About the Author

Avian care and behavior consultant Nikki Moustaki has authored numerous books on birds and their care and training. She has also written for many national magazines and has been featured on television and radio shows.

Nikki has been involved with birds since 1988, eventually becoming active in local bird clubs and later breeding and showing birds. During those first few years, she kept lovebirds, cockatiels, budgies, lories, macaws, Amazons, conures, finches, canaries, and brotergeris. Around 1993, she became aware of the bird overpopulation problem, stopped breeding, and began helping in various national rescue efforts. Today, she lives in New York City with an African grey parrot, a Meyer's parrot, lovebirds, and two schnauzers. She hosts the website www.goodbird.com.

Photo Credits

Parakeets